LIFESPAN
INVESTING

LIFESPAN INVESTING

BUILDING THE BEST PORTFOLIO
FOR EVERY STAGE OF YOUR LIFE

CLIFFORD PISTOLESE

McGraw-Hill

New York   Chicago   San Francisco   Lisbon   London
Madrid   Mexico City   Milan   New Delhi   San Juan
Seoul   Singapore   Sydney   Toronto

1 2 3 4 5 6 7 8 9 0 FGR/FGR 0 9 8 7

ISBN-13: 978-0-07-149811-1
ISBN-10: 0-07-149811-7

This publication is designed to provide accurate and authoritative information in regard to the subject matter covered. It is sold with the understanding that neither the author nor the publisher is engaged in rendering legal, accounting, or other professional service. If legal advice or other expert assistance is required, the services of a competent professional person should be sought.

—From a Declaration of Principles jointly adopted by a Committee of the American Bar Association and a Committee of Publishers

McGraw-Hill books are available at special quantity discounts to use as premiums and sales promotions, or for use in corporate training programs. For more information, please write to the Director of Special Sales, Professional Publishing, McGraw-Hill, Two Penn Plaza, New York, NY 10121-2298. Or contact your local bookstore.

Library of Congress Cataloging-in-Publication Data
Pistolese, Clifford.
   Lifespan investing : building the best portfolio for every state of your life / by Clifford Pistolese.
      p. cm.
   ISBN-13: 978-0-07-149811-1 (hardcover : alk. paper)
   ISBN-10: 0-07-149811-7
   1. Portfolio management.   2. Finance, Personal.   3. Wealth.   I. Title.
   HG4529.5.P57   2007
   332.6—dc22

                                                                    2007 14005

This book is dedicated to you, the investor, willing to work, save, and invest to achieve financial independence. This attitude of self-reliance will enable you to have a comfortable retirement even if the Social Security program or company pension plan payments are not there for you when the time comes. By using the long-term investment plan presented in this book, you can create the wealth to finance an enjoyable lifestyle in retirement.

CONTENTS

PREFACE

If you are concerned that you may not have enough money to finance a comfortable retirement, this book presents a way to solve that problem. It contains a long-term investment strategy to maximize the amount of wealth you will accumulate in your lifetime. It also contains the research procedures to find and evaluate each potential investment. By taking this studious approach to the subject matter and being willing to devote time and effort over the years, you will reach your financial objective.

The focus of this book is on how to take maximum advantage of the opportunities in the stock market. You will learn how to make superior capital gains in bull markets and how to preserve those gains during bear markets. You will also learn how to create a strong income flow during range-bound markets. And you will learn how to diversify your portfolio among different types of investments to control the level of risk.

The first two chapters of the book present information about fundamental and technical analysis. Fundamental analysis is the evaluation of a company's ability to run its business effectively to maximize earnings consistently. Technical analysis is the interpretation of a company's charted stock price pattern to decide when to buy, how long to hold, and when to sell. Chapter 3 explains the concept and the process of portfolio management. This involves setting your financial objective for retirement; selecting investments to meet that objective; and rebalancing your portfolio to make it appropriate for each stage in your life.

Each of the remaining chapters presents three suggested portfolios. One is for use during bull markets, another is for bear markets, and the third applies when the market fluctuates in a trading range.

The analytical technique you learn in Chapter 2 will enable you to see which of these phases the market is in. Making these observations accurately is one of the keys to investing successfully.

If you have never read a book organized like this one, here's a suggested approach to take. Read the first three chapters to acquire the concepts of fundamental analysis, technical analysis, and portfolio management. Then read the chapter that pertains to your age group and decide how you want to start implementing your investment strategy. Follow up by reading the later chapters to get an overview of the plan for multiplying your assets over your lifetime. Finally, reading the earlier chapters will provide additional helpful points of information.

NOTE

This book is not intended to assist in day trading. Nor is it applicable to making quick trades for small profits. Instead, it contains a long-term strategy for building wealth during your working lifetime and for preserving it after you retire.

LIFESPAN INVESTING

Chapter 1

Fundamental Analysis

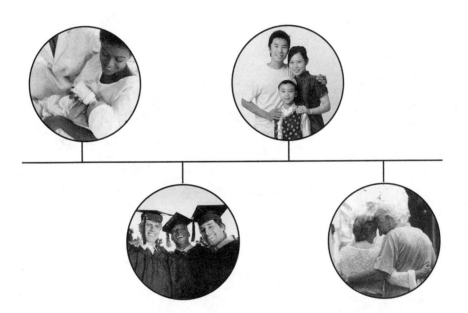

Introduction

Fundamental analysis is the process of conducting research into a company's operations and financial condition to determine its quality as an investment. You can also use this analytic procedure to assess the suitability of the investment for you.

If you are an aggressive investor, does the company have the potential growth that will provide a large capital gain? If you are conservative, does the company have management that will produce consistent profitable performance? If you are seeking income flow, does the company have a record of paying high dividends? By conducting research to find the answers to these questions, you will be able to make investments that are appropriate for you. In the following sections I have presented an overview of how to evaluate a company's operations, financial condition, earnings record, and competitive position.

Geographic Reach

A major consideration in assessing a company's worthiness as an investment is the geographic reach of its business operations. Does it conduct its business locally, regionally, nationally, or on a global basis? Companies with operations in many different countries have a better chance of maintaining a strong flow of revenue because of the many diversified markets into which they sell their products and services.

Consequently, companies that have global merchandizing and name recognition have a competitive advantage over those who sell to a local, regional, or national market. As the process of globalization continues, companies who can take advantage of this trend have the best prospects for success.

The Interbrand Corporation, which assesses the impact and recognition of companies globally, reports that the most widely known brand name is Coca-Cola. Its impressive global presence helps it maintain the dominant position in the business of selling soft drinks, noncarbonated beverages, sports drinks, syrups, and concentrates.

There are many other companies that also have the advantages of selling into markets beyond our national borders. Some of the best-known international or global companies are listed here, along with their stock symbols and brief descriptions of their businesses.

- Toyota (TM) has the objective of becoming the largest maker of cars, pickup trucks, and sport utility vehicles.
- McDonald's (MCD) is the largest, most widely patronized fast-food restaurant.
- Google (GOOG) is the premier Internet search engine. It is expanding into related Internet enterprises.
- Nike (NKE) is the international leader in the casual and sports apparel business. It is endorsed by high-profile sports figures.
- Kellogg (K) is the leader in the breakfast cereals business. It produces cereals that appeal to both adults and children.
- Apple Computer (AAPL) is known internationally for its computers, mobile music players, and other electronic devices. Its logo of an apple is universally recognized and respected.
- Colgate Palmolive (CL) has worldwide acceptance of its lines of personal care products.
- Caterpillar (CAT) provides quick service to keep its construction equipment and engines operating around the world. It is known universally by its nickname, "Cat."
- Cummins (CMI) sells and services diesel engines and electric power generation systems in 160 countries.
- Starbucks (SBUX) is the most successful retailer of coffee-based specialty drinks. Its stores also provide music, books, access to the Internet, and other features to appeal to its customers.
- Symantic (SYMC) is the leader in Internet security for personal computers.

The Finance.Yahoo.com Web site has information specifying where each company has operations. To find out, enter the stock symbol of the company you are researching. Click on Profile in the menu on the left and scroll down to read a description of the company's operations.

Some of the information presented above has been derived from research done by, or on behalf of, *Business Week* magazine.

Earnings Growth

The ability to increase earnings consistently over a period of years is an achievement that appeals to many types of investors: aggressive, conservative, and income oriented. To qualify for the list shown below, each company had to increase earnings by more than 75 percent for a period of three years. This outstanding performance is evidence they have been very efficient and profitable. The following are the names of the companies, their stock symbols, and a brief description of their businesses.

- Palomar Medical Technologies (PMTI) makes and markets lasers and lamp systems for medical and cosmetic procedures.
- VASCO Data Security (VDSI) designs and services identification systems and other online security measures for Internet service providers.
- Blue Nile (NILE) offers a comprehensive selection of diamonds and other precious gems for sale on the Internet.
- Wayside Technology (WSTG) wholesales software and hardware to professionals in the field of information technology.
- Imperial Industries (IPII) produces and distributes stucco and other construction materials.

- Amedisys (AMED) provides home health care for invalids and hospice services for the terminally ill.
- Netflix (NFLX) is an online DVD rental company that delivers movies and doesn't charge for late returns.
- Hurco (HURC) makes and sells industrial software and equipment for machining and metalworking.
- Encore Wire (WIRE) makes and sells electrical copper wire and cable.
- LoJack (LOJN) makes transmitters that are placed in vehicles to help police locate those that are stolen.
- eCollege.com (ECLG) sells college-level courses to students for home study via the Internet.
- Concur Technologies (CNQR) streamlines corporate expense management to save clients money.
- Kforce (KFRC) finds employees for companies that need specialists in finance, technology, medicine, and science.

NOTE

Before purchasing shares of any company on this list, access its recent earnings history to see what the current trend is. This information is available from the Web site Finance.Yahoo.com. Select Income Statement at the bottom of the menu. Scroll down the statement and read the data showing the net income available to the common stock. Check the three-year record of earnings to see if the company is continuing to increase its earnings.

Evaluating Stock Prices

Reading the price of a company's stock in the newspaper or on the ticker tape is not the best way of determining whether the price of the stock is low, medium, or high. To assess the price of a company's stock, a more financially relevant method is to calculate the price-to-earnings ratio (P/E). The P/E ratio is obtained by dividing the current stock price by the earnings per share for the past year. For example, if a company earned $10 per share and its stock is priced at $100 per share, it has a P/E ratio of 100 divided by 10, which is a ratio of 10 to 1. A company's P/E ratio is regarded as reasonable if it is about the same level as its rate of earnings growth. Therefore, if a company is increasing its earnings by 15 percent per year, a P/E ratio of about 15 to 1 would be appropriate. If the P/E ratio was 10 to 1 or less, it would be low. If the P/E ratio was 20 to 1 or more, it would be high.

In the following list are companies that had average yearly profit growth rates of 20 to 30 percent for a three-year time period. As of the date of publication, these companies had P/E ratios lower than their growth rates. Here are their names, stock symbols, and descriptions of their businesses.

- Brigham Exploration (BEXP) uses three-dimensional seismic technology to explore for oil and natural gas.
- Miller Industries (MLR) manufactures bodies for towing and recovery vehicles.
- Parlux Fragrances (PARL) produces and distributes name-brand perfumes.
- Sun Hydraulics (SNHY) produces screw-in hydraulic cartridge valves and manifolds.
- Unit (UNT) explores for oil and natural gas in North America.
- VSE (VSEC) provides engineering and technical help for government systems.
- Gevity HR (GVHR) performs the functions of a human resources department for corporations.
- EFJ (EFI) makes and distributes analog and digital wireless radio systems.
- OmniVision Technologies (OVTI) sells image sensor chips for digital cameras and security systems.
- PeopleSupport (PSPT) outsources customer care, technical support, and sales.

The current stock price and P/E ratios are available on the Web site Finance.Yahoo.com. Read the Summary display to get this information. While low P/E ratios are generally preferable, sometimes higher ratios are justified because the company's rate of earnings growth is accelerating.

Competitive Situation

Whether a company succeeds, fails, or has moderate success depends not only on its own ability and efforts but also on the competitive situation. The business environment is conducive to growth in an industry that is expanding because of high demand for the products and services the businesses sell. Another favorable factor is if there is a barrier to new entrants into the industry. For example, TETRA Technologies (TTI) maintains, repairs, and decommissions oil- and gas-drilling platforms. Skilled technicians who can perform these operations are very hard to find and recruit. Consequently, potential competitors are restrained from entering the industry and starting up competitive operations.

Also, TETRA Technologies has a large backlog of work because demand for its services runs ahead of its ability to deliver completed projects. With the competitive advantages these conditions create, this company can raise prices on new contracts. This means the company will probably increase its earnings in the future.

Large rewards can come from buying stock in a company that has an established competitive advantage. Another positive factor is if a company is much bigger than its competitors or has a leading position in its industry through technological superiority. Listed here are some companies that have one or more of these desirable characteristics.

- Boeing (BA) is a leader in the manufacture of commercial aircraft and aerospace systems.

- Cameco (CCJ) is the largest producer and processor of uranium for nuclear power plants and other applications.
- Mattel (MAT) markets dolls, toy vehicles, games, puzzles, children's books, learning toys, and child restraint seats for cars. Its products are distributed worldwide.
- Dril-Quip (DRQ) leads the industry in providing underwater services to install and maintain oil and natural gas drilling rigs.
- Altria (MO) is the largest producer of tobacco products for worldwide markets.
- Becton Dickinson (BDX) leads in the sale of medical supplies, laboratory equipment, and diagnostic machines.
- Laboratory Corporation of America (LH) has a leadership position in providing testing services to the medical profession.
- GameStop (GME) leads in the retailing of video games and software for personal computers. It has stores in the United States, Canada, Europe, and Australia.
- Joy Global (JOYG) leads in the sale and servicing of machines for mining coal and other minerals worldwide.
- Abaxis (ABAX) leads in marketing portable blood analysis systems to medical doctors and veterinarians.
- Anixter International (AXE) is the leading wholesale distributor of a wide variety of electronics and equipment worldwide.
- Ceradyne (CRDN) leads in the marketing of ceramic products, powders, and components for defense and industrial applications.
- Garmin (GRMN) is the leading producer and marketer of global positioning systems (GPS) for a wide variety of applications.
- Deere (DE) dominates the farm equipment industry and has worldwide operations.
- American Reprographics (ARP) leads in the provision of document management services for architectural, engineering, and construction companies.

- Fastenal (FAST) is the leading company in the production, distribution, and marketing of fasteners, nuts, and bolts.
- Valero Energy (VLO) has the largest refinery capacity in North America. It produces gasoline, distillates, jet fuel, asphalt, petrochemicals, and lubricants.
- General Dynamics (GD) is a leading supplier of nuclear submarines, combat vehicles, and satellites.
- Safeway (SWY) is a leader in the supermarket industry with a growing natural foods business. It also owns a very profitable gift card company.
- Quest Diagnostics (DGX) is a leading provider of laboratory testing and diagnostic equipment and services.
- American Standard (ASD) is a leading supplier of building materials, kitchen components, bathroom fixtures, air-conditioning systems, and vehicle control equipment.
- Vulcan Materials (VMC) is a leading producer of the aggregate materials used in building highways.
- Pall Corporation (PLL) is the leading producer of filters and separators for medical, industrial, and research applications. It is the largest in the industry and has worldwide operations.

NOTE

The competitive relationships in all industries is subject to change. Before making a purchase, you should conduct a search to get current information on whether a company still has its competitive advantage. To do this research, go to the Web site Finance.Yahoo.com and click on menu item Competitors.

Company Finances

In the preceding sections we looked at companies from the perspective of global reach, earnings growth, relative level of the stock price, and competitive situation. In the following sections we will focus on criteria by which the financial condition of companies can be evaluated.

Profit Margins

The profit margin of a corporation is an important statistic for evaluating the ability of its management team to conduct the operations efficiently and profitably. The profit margin is the percent of profit remaining after subtracting expenses and costs from the company's revenue. Achieving a profit margin of 15 percent or higher is evidence that the company is controlling expenses and costs well. Listed below are companies that meet that criterion with their stock symbols, profit margins, and descriptions of their businesses.

Company Stock	Symbol	Profit Margin %
Microsoft	(MSFT)	28

Produces software for a wide variety of technical applications in computers and other electronic devices.

Citigroup	(C)	31

Is a large U.S. investment bank with offices around the world.

Oracle	(ORCL)	23

Is a major producer of the software that facilitates the operation of the Internet.

Johnson & Johnson	(JNJ)	21

Is a major supplier of medical supplies and equipment.

Cisco	(CSCO)	19

Sells networking and communications products and services for the transportation of data, voice, and video.

(continues on next page)

Company Stock	Symbol	Profit Margin %
Intel	(INTC)	18

Is a leading producer of the internal components of computers and other Internet-related devices.

Harley-Davidson	(HOG)	16

Produces a variety of motorcycles and related clothing and accessories to support the on-the-road lifestyle.

Hittite Microwave	(HITT)	30

Its integrated circuits are used in cable modems, satellites, and many other electronic devices.

Dynamic Materials	(BOOM)	20

Produces explosion-welded clad metal plates and other metallic assemblies.

ADTRAN	(ADTN)	19

Develops and supplies products used in Internet and other telecommunications systems.

Gen-Probe	(GPRO)	18

Makes equipment that can rapidly identify germs and diseases.

AMN Health Care	(AHS)	16

Provides registered nurses to hospitals, nursing homes, and other organizations in need of skilled nursing care.

NOTE

This information came from the Standard & Poor's Compustat database of more than 10,000 publicly traded corporations. This data reflects a time period prior to the publication of this book. To get current profit margin data on a company, refer to the Web site Finance.Yahoo.com and click on the menu item Key Statistics.

Income Statements

Publicly held corporations are required to file quarterly income statements with the Securities and Exchange Commission and with the stock exchange on which they are listed. These statements give stockholders information on how well company management has handled the finances during the preceding year or quarter.

Prior to purchasing a company's stock, review its most recent income statement to evaluate its financial performance. This can be done by going to the Finance.Yahoo.com Web site and clicking on the menu item Income Statement. Check the following items.

- The amount of revenue taken in during the time period. (This is usually referred to as the "Top Line.")
- The costs associated with the collection of that revenue is subtracted and the result is the gross profit.
- From the gross profit, expenses such as maintenance, salaries, advertising, and administrative costs are subtracted. The result is the operating income.
- Finally, interest payments, taxes, and other recurring and nonrecurring items are subtracted to get the net income applicable to the common shares. (This is referred to as the "Bottom Line.")

After reviewing the net income for the last quarter, you can compare it to previous quarters and to the same quarter of the preceding year. Note whether the quarterly net income has been rising or falling or if there have been any losses in the past year. The most desirable situation is a record of rising income and no losses. Thousands of company income statements are available from Finance.Yahoo.com and from other Web sites.

Debt Levels

Some companies have no debt. Other companies have too much debt. One of the important tasks of management is to determine which level of debt is appropriate to meet the needs the company may have for expansion or other operational goals. A debt level of zero is appropriate if the company is generating enough income to finance its growth objectives. A low level of debt (less than cash on hand) usually indicates the company is doing a good job of financing its operations. But taking on excessive debt (much higher than cash on hand) raises the risk level.

Very high levels of debt can result in bankruptcy when the income of the company declines and interest payments on the borrowed money can't be made. This situation may develop during a recession in the economy or when severe competitive conditions develop in the industry. Check the company's debt level before purchasing its stock to decide if you can tolerate the risk involved.

Companies in some industries need to borrow money in order to finance their businesses. Electric utilities take on high levels of debt to finance the huge infrastructure needed to produce electricity. This can be done without much risk of default because their customers must pay for the electric they use. Therefore, these companies have a reliable revenue stream from which to pay the interest to the lender.

Industrial manufacturing companies also have huge infrastructures to finance. But the revenue these companies generate is not as dependable as that of utilities. It is not as reliable because their customers are not compelled to buy the manufactured products. They can delay purchases or switch to alternative suppliers.

The determination of what is a reasonable level of debt varies widely among industries. To decide if the debt level of a company is justifiable, compare it to the debt level of other companies in that industry. If a company's debt is higher and its profit margin is lower than the other companies, the profits may be depressed by the drain of having to make payments on the loans. On the other hand, if a company has a lower level of debt than others in that business and the profit margin is higher, it usually indicates management is using the loans productively. Thus if the debt level is appropriate, there can be a positive effect on the profit margin. Conversely, if the debt level is too high, it will have a negative effect. Review and evaluate the debt level before purchasing stock in any company.

Return on Investment

A basic question in fundamental analysis is, how do you get an acceptable return on your investment? Your return comes in the form of capital gains and dividends. Over the years this combination can be a powerful producer of wealth. Investors who get high returns on their investments learn how to identify the companies that can produce outstanding results. Those companies have the following characteristics.

- Positive brand-name recognition
- Operations in worldwide markets
- Strong financial condition
- Consistent increases in earnings
- Low price-to-earnings ratios
- Competitive advantages
- Manageable levels of debt

Receiving dividends is the most immediate form of return on investment. Companies that pay dividends return more to the investor over the long run. Dividends are the stockholders' reward for being patient while waiting for capital gains. The ideal investment is a company that pays a dividend and produces a large capital gain.

The payment of dividends is optional with the board of directors of the company. A record of dividend payments is available at Finance.Yahoo.com. Click on menu item Historical Prices and then on Dividends Only. By reviewing the resulting display, you will see the dollar value of the dividends paid during the preceding years. You will also see if any payment has been omitted. This review gives you an indication of how reliable the company is in making payments to stockholders. It also reveals whether they have been increasing the dollar value of the dividends.

NOTE

This chapter has provided an overview of fundamental analysis. For a more detailed review of this subject area, refer to the books on this topic in Appendix D, "Bibliography."

Chapter 2

Technical Analysis

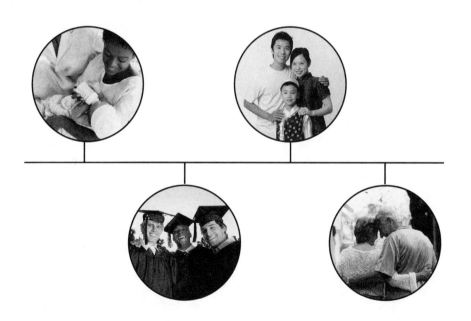

Introduction

When the demand for shares of a stock is greater than the supply, the price goes up. When the supply of shares is greater than the demand, the price goes down. As these price movements occur over a period of time, they form a wide variety of patterns. Technical analysis is the method for understanding the implications of those stock price patterns. In this chapter you will see some of the most common patterns and learn how to interpret them. You will learn about the significance of changes in the volume of trading. And the relationships between stock prices and their moving averages will be illustrated and explained.

Fundamental analysis provides information for determining what to buy. That's the first half of researching an investment. Technical analysis completes the process. It helps you decide when to buy, how long to hold, and when to sell. Used together, fundamental and technical analyses provide a comprehensive approach for making information-based, objective investment decisions about buying and selling stocks.

Notes

The patterns shown in this chapter have been idealized for easy interpretation. Actual price charts contain these patterns and many other formations. It will take some time and study to become skilled in the interpretation of price patterns. If you are willing to make the effort, acquiring the ability to interpret stock price patterns will be a valuable aid toward becoming a more successful investor.

This chapter provides an overview of some basic concepts of technical analysis. For a more detailed review of the subject, additional reference sources are listed in Appendix D, "Bibliography."

Common Price Patterns

Learning to recognize common bottom patterns is important because they often indicate the start of a bull market. Each bottom pattern has different variations. This is why it will require some practice to distinguish a significant pattern from the many random price movements.

Double Bottom

One of the important patterns to recognize is the double bottom. (See Chart 2.1.) This type of bottom develops because investors who

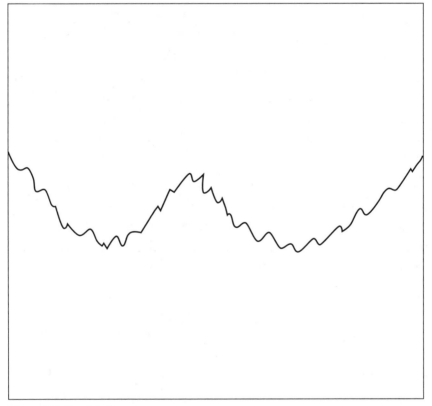

Chart 2.1 Double Bottom

didn't buy at the first bottom don't want to miss a chance to buy at that low level again.

A double bottom can form within a few weeks or can take the better part of a year to develop. This pattern provides a warning that the future price trend will be up. A buy signal is given when the price rise up from the second bottom surpasses the peak price in between the two bottoms. A double bottom pattern implies a rise in price to much higher levels.

Inverted Head and Shoulders

The inverted head and shoulders pattern often marks the beginning of a major bull market. (See Chart 2.2.) This pattern usually takes the

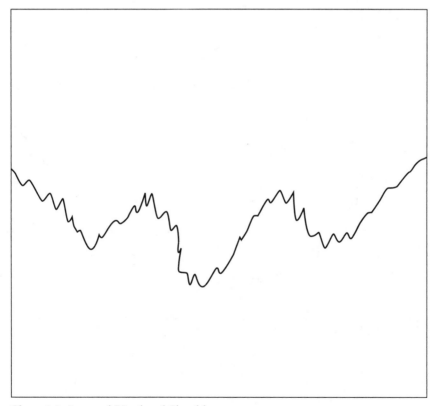

Chart 2.2 Inverted Head and Shoulders

major part of a year to form. Either shoulder may be at a different level than the other and unlike the inverted human shape it crudely portrays, there may be more than one shoulder on either or both sides of the head. The time to buy is when the final rise has surpassed the highest peak within the pattern. Then you can enjoy riding the bull to the top of the market advance.

Rounding Bottom

A rounding bottom is a formation that gradually converts a down-trend into an uptrend. (See Chart 2.3.) The lowest section is the ac-cumulation phase. This buying is done by knowledgeable investors

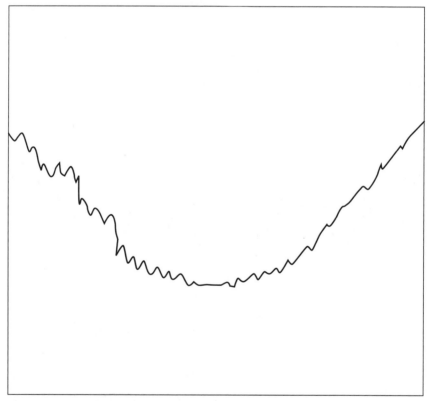

Chart 2.3 Rounding Bottom

who realize the stock is selling at extreme bargain levels, and they buy all the shares that are offered. As the supply of stock for sale declines, the price momentum shifts to the upside. After an uptrend becomes established, a large long-term capital gain is likely to be your reward for recognizing this saucer-shaped formation.

Upward Price Trend

An uptrend is defined by a series of ascending short-term bottoms. (See Chart 2.4.) Uptrends that rise at angles of 10 to 30 degrees are sustainable for the long term. Ascent angles between 30 and 45 degrees are sustainable for an intermediate period. Higher angles of as-

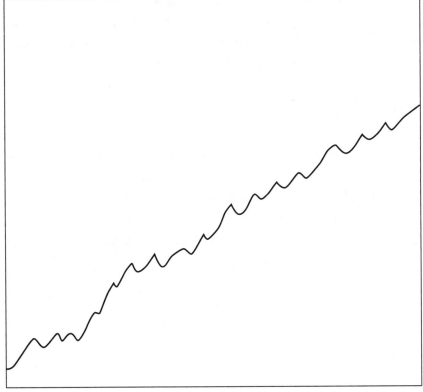

Chart 2.4 Upward Price Trend

cent are usually short lived, but can produce very large paper profits quickly. Unfortunately, such steep uptrends often reverse without warning and the price becomes susceptible to a free fall.

NOTE

The angles of ascent referred to are based on a chart with a time span of one year. A longer time span makes the angle of ascent look steeper. A shorter time span makes the angle appear more gradual. All charts shown in this book represent a time span of one year.

Common Top Patterns

After a long uptrend has exhausted itself, a top pattern often appears. These patterns are most likely to be a double top, a head and shoulders top, or a rounding top. They usually signal the end of the bull market and the start of a bear market. But sometimes the sequel will be a horizontal range-bound market.

Double Top

It's important to recognize when a double top is forming because this pattern is a warning that the end of a bull market is approaching. (See Chart 2.5.) The sell signal is given when the price declines below the intervening bottom. The two tops can be at the same height or at slightly different levels. When you see a double top forming, be ready to take any paper profits you may have.

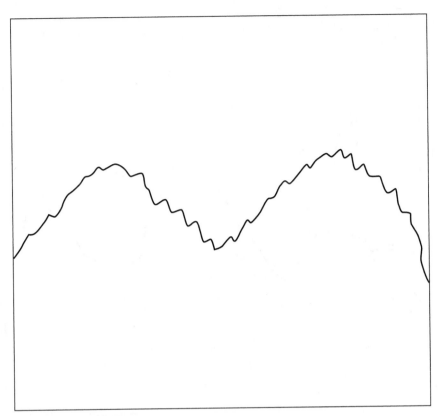

Chart 2.5 Double Top

Head and Shoulders

The head and shoulders pattern indicates that a bull market has exhausted itself. (See Chart 2.6.) The peak of the advance is the top of the head where buyers were willing to pay the highest prices. The shoulders may be unequal in height and there may be more than one on either side. The indication to sell is when the decline from the right shoulder goes below the lowest point in the pattern.

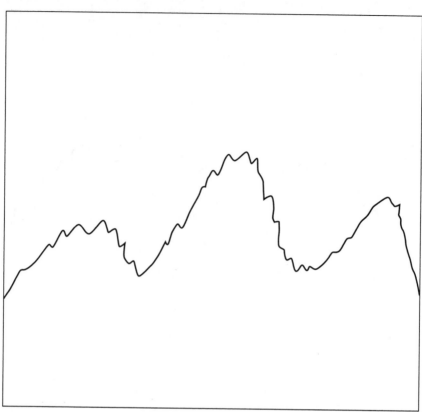

Chart 2.6 Head and Shoulders Top

Rounding Top

A rounding top is a formation that converts a long-term uptrend into a downtrend. (See Chart 2.7.) The center of the top is the distribution phase where knowledgeable stockholders sell their shares to buyers willing to pay top dollar. Most of these patterns are smooth and resemble an upside-down saucer. But some of them are jagged and difficult to recognize. Whether they are smooth or not, the meaning is the same. When the downtrend becomes established, be prepared to convert your paper profits into capital gains.

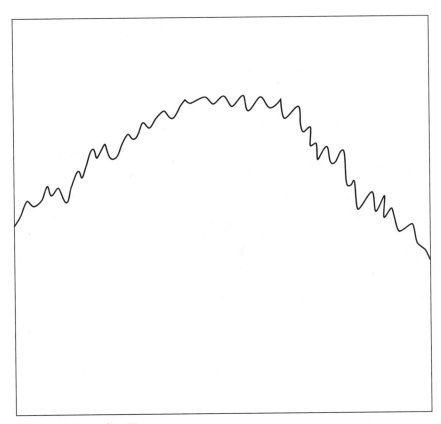

Chart 2.7 Rounding Top

From Uptrend to Downtrend

Sometimes a bull market changes into a bear market without an intervening extended pattern. In this case an uptrend is converted directly into a downtrend. This development can occur when some unexpected bad news is announced and surprises everyone. Or it may indicate that the market has become extremely overbought due to "irrational exuberance," a phrase made famous by Alan Greenspan, a former chairman of the Federal Reserve. The sell signal is given when the price breaks down through its 200-day moving average. (See Chart 2.8.)

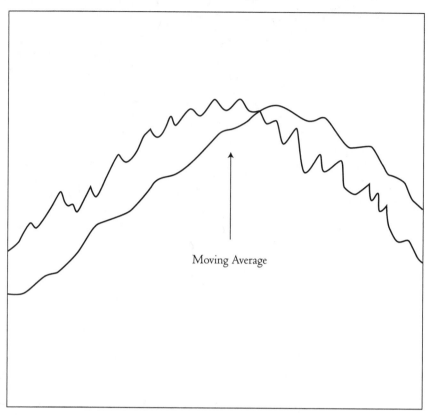

Moving Average

Chart 2.8 From Uptrend to Downtrend

Trading Range

The price of a stock can get stuck in a trading range when supply and demand are relatively equal. (See Chart 2.9.) The top of the range is determined by a resistance level which is the price where stockholders are eager to sell. The bottom is a support level where potential buyers believe the price is a great bargain. As long as both buyers and sellers are convinced they are right, the price remains within the range. Some active traders try to profit from this situation by buying at the bottom of the range and selling near the top. However, this tactic involves some risks as will be explained below.

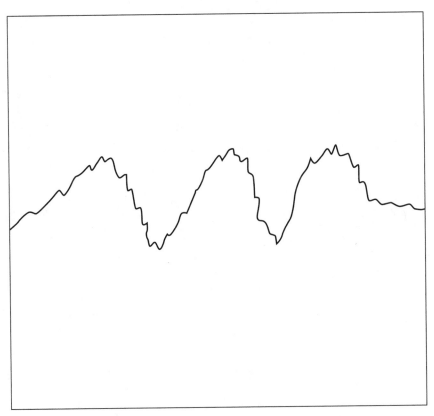

Chart 2.9 Trading Range

Breakout above Resistance

Trading ranges can last a long time, but not forever. Eventually a breakout occurs either to the upside or the downside. (See Chart 2.10.) A breakout to the upside occurs when the company does something which convinces the stockholders that the prospects have improved very significantly. They decide to stop selling and hold their shares in the expectation of much higher prices. Potential buyers are also convinced by the company's action that the price will go higher, and they are then willing to buy above the resistance level. This strong increase in demand causes the breakout to the upside and creates an uptrend. Those traders who have been selling at the resistance level

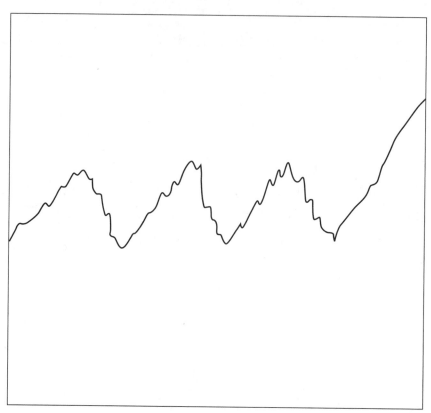

Chart 2.10 Trading Range Breakout to Upside

miss out on this advance, having sold just before the beginning of the uptrend.

Breakout below Support

A breakout down through the support level occurs when something negative happens and the support level price is no longer considered to be a bargain. (See Chart 2.11.) The stockholders become anxious to sell because of the bad news. With the lessened demand from buyers and increased supply from the stockholders, the price penetrates the support level and goes into a downtrend. The traders who were buying near the support level are then holding a stock which is prob-

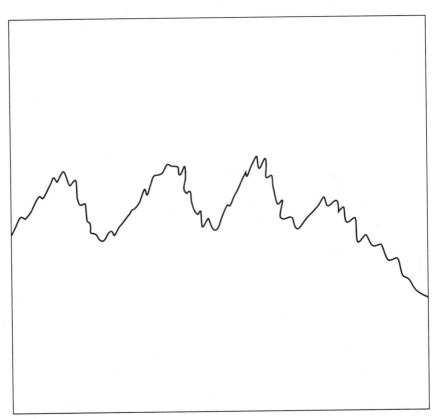

Chart 2.11 Trading Range Breakout to Downside

ably going to decline a large distance. That is the risk of buying a stock when it is at the bottom of a trading range.

Ascending Triangle

An ascending triangle is a contest in which buyers are more eager than sellers. (See Chart 2-12.) The sellers are convinced a particular price is a good place to sell, and this creates a resistance level which forms the top side of the triangle. The buyers become more eager to own the stock, and they are willing to pay higher and higher prices. This results in an uptrend line which is the lower side of the triangle.

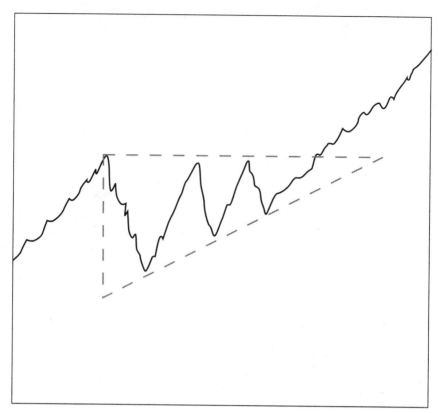

Chart 2.12 Ascending Triangle

Because of the increasing buying pressure, the breakout is almost always to the upside. The size of the price rise is likely to be equal to or greater than the height of the triangle. Occasionally some unexpected news event reverses the relationship between supply and demand, and the price goes down through the uptrend line. Therefore, it is better to buy only after the price has penetrated up through the resistance level.

Symmetrical Triangle

A symmetrical triangle forms when stockholders who want to sell and investors who want to buy are equally eager. A downtrend forms the upper side of the triangle as stockholders become more anxious to sell. An uptrend forms as the bottom of the triangle as buyers are equally anxious. At some point either the buyers or the sellers prove to be right and the price breaks out to the upside or downside. A clue as to which side will win can be detected from the direction of entry into

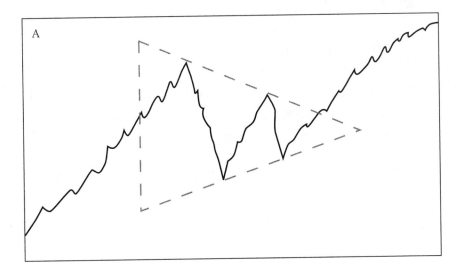

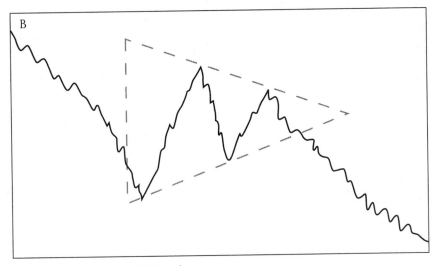

Chart 2.13 Symmetrical Triangles

the triangle. If the trend before the triangle formed was to the upside, the breakout is likely to be in that direction. (See Chart 2-13A.) If the price was in a downtrend before the triangle formed, the breakout is likely to be to the downside. (See Chart 2-13B.) In either case, the subsequent rise or fall in price is usually equal to, or greater than, the height of the triangle.

Descending Triangle

A descending triangle represents an unequal contest, with the sellers being more eager than the buyers. (See Chart 2-14.) The buyers are convinced a particular price is a great bargain. They buy consistently

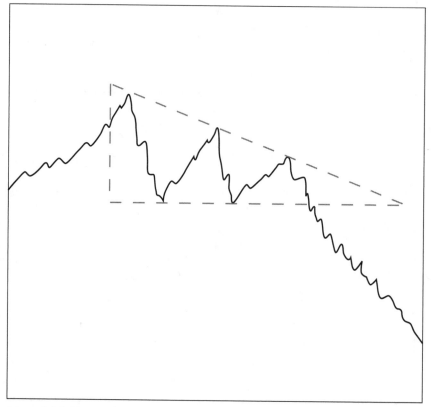

Chart 2.14 Descending Triangle

at that price and form a support level. The stockholders are willing to sell at lower and lower prices and a downtrend becomes the top of the triangle. Most of the time the price breakout is to the downside. When it goes through the support level, it will usually decline a distance equal to, or more than, the height of the triangle.

Increased Volume Confirms Uptrend

Fluctuations in the volume of trading in a stock provide clues to the sustainability of a stock price movement. An expansion in the trading volume validates the price movement. Increases in the volume of trading reflects the enthusiasm of the investors who are buying the shares. If a stock price starts rising and there is little or no increase in the volume traded, it is unlikely that the rise will be sustained. Before making an investment in a stock, look for a recent and continuing increase in the volume of trading to ensure the uptrend is likely to continue. (See Chart 2.15.)

Increased Volume Confirms Breakout

In order to establish a trading range, a stock price must have failed to penetrate the resistance level several times. The strength of the demand and supply forces has been balanced for some time. To break out of the range to the upside, a large increase in trading volume is needed. When the price does break out above the resistance level, check the amount of increase in the volume. An increase of more than 100 percent provides assurance that the advance can continue a significant distance. (See Chart 2.16.)

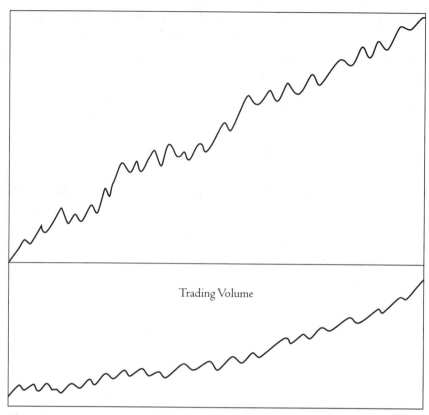

Trading Volume

Chart 2.15 Increasing Trading Volume Confirms Uptrend

Moving Average

The moving average of a stock price is the average of a consecutive series of closing prices. For example, a 200-day moving average is the average of closing prices for the most recent 200 business days. Tomorrow the oldest price will be dropped from the calculation and today's closing price will be included. Moving averages of varying lengths are shown in stock price charts on Web sites that focus on the stock market. The moving average for 200 days is the one preferred by long-term investors. Active traders prefer shorter averages because they are more appropriate for making frequent trading decisions.

Chart 2.16 Increased Trading Volume Confirms Breakout

Charts 2.17 through 2.20 show the main significant relationships between stock prices and their 200-day moving averages.

Price Falls through Moving Average

A stock price leads its moving average because the price is current whereas the moving average includes past data. (See Chart 2.17.) The moving average smooths out the daily fluctuations of the price and more accurately shows the direction in which the price is moving. Chart 2.17 shows a stock price and its 200-day moving average in uptrends for a while. Notice that the stock price has recently fallen through the moving average. This change in relationship indicates a

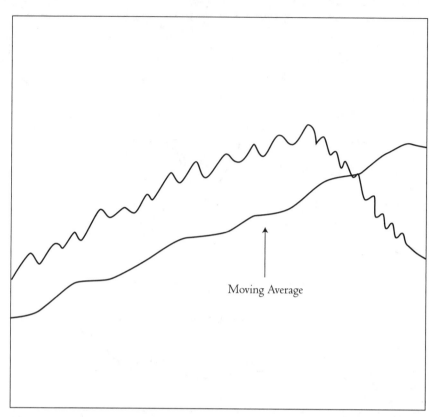

Moving Average

Chart 2.17 Stock Price Falls Through Moving Average

switch in momentum from up to down. Stockholders should take this downward penetration as a signal to sell and preserve any capital gains they may have.

Price Rises above Moving Average

Here the stock price has been fluctuating below the 200-day moving average which has been rising slowly for a while. (See Chart 2.18.) Based on some good news about the company, the stock has penetrated up through the moving average. This shows a switch in momentum to the upside. This change in relationship may be taken as a buy signal.

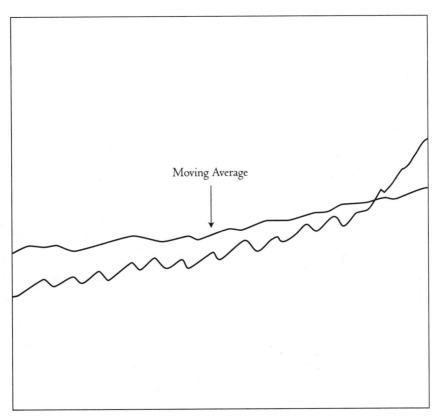

Moving Average

Chart 2.18 Stock Price Rises above Moving Average

Price Leads Moving Average Down

Chart 2.19 shows a very negative situation. The stock price is leading the 200-day moving average downward. This relationship indicates the stock is in a confirmed downtrend. There is nothing in this relationship to make a technical analyst believe the momentum will change for the better. This is the type of pattern investors should take as a danger sign because it illustrates negative momentum resulting in continuing paper losses to shareholders.

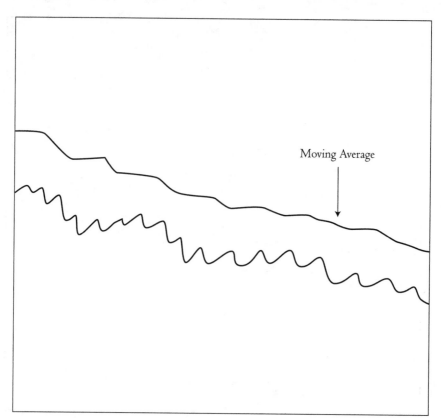

Moving Average

Chart 2.19 Stock Price Leads Moving Average Down

Price Leads Moving Average Up

Chart 2.20 shows the ideal relationship between a stock price and its 200-day moving average. The price and the moving average are rising at an angle of approximately 30 degrees. This angle of ascent is sustainable for the long term so a large gain is likely to result. As you do research on various stocks, this is the pattern to look for as an indication of capital gains to come.

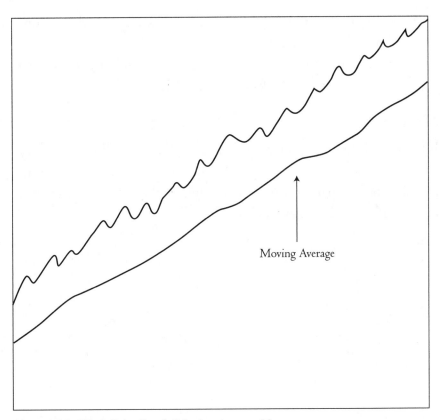

Chart 2.20 Stock Price Leads Moving Average Up

Research Procedure

When you conduct your technical analysis of stock price patterns, here is a research procedure to evaluate the relationship between the stock price and its 200-day moving average.

- Go to StockCharts.com. Press the drop down menu icon and select Gallery View.
- Enter a stock symbol in the search slot and click Go.
- View the daily chart and scroll down to see the weekly chart. The charts show a 200-day or a 40-week moving average (40 business day weeks equals 200 days).

- Look for stock and moving average relationships like the one shown in Chart 2.20.
- If you can't find any that look like Chart 2.20, a good second choice is one that looks like Chart 2.18.

NOTE

Internet Web sites are subject to change. If you can't follow this or any other sequence exactly, explore the site and find what you want through another path. Or refer to another of the Web sites described in Appendix C, "Internet Resources."

Chapter 3

Portfolio Management

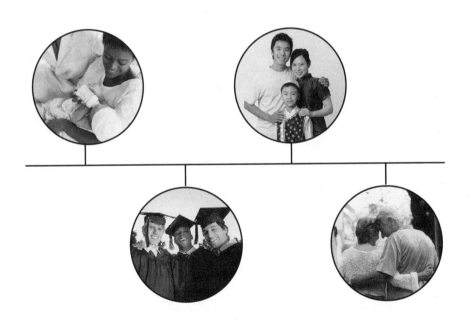

Introduction

Investing with a lifetime perspective is the logical and most effective way to prepare for a financially sound retirement. Individuals who practice the habits of saving and investing have the best prospects for achieving wealth by the time they retire. People who delay starting an investment plan will likely have a low-budget retirement. Those who depend on the Social Security program or a company pension plan may find the funds inadequate. They may have to continue working as long as they are able. To avoid this situation, build your portfolio as suggested in this book and your retirement will be well financed and enjoyable.

This chapter provides an overview of a strategy for managing your portfolio. Subsequent chapters describe the types of investments appropriate for each five-year period in an adult lifetime. Procedures for getting helpful, valuable information from Internet Web sites will also be provided.

Portfolio Management Strategy

The portfolio management strategy presented in this book evolves through the following major stages.

Stage I

In the time period between the ages of 20 and 35 the objective is to achieve maximum capital appreciation by taking elevated, but reasonable, risks. In these early years, young investors need to purchase stock in small companies that have fast revenue and earnings growth and high profit margins. Companies expanding their operations in young and growing industries provide the best opportunities. The information in Chapters 4, 5, and 6 will help you find companies with these characteristics.

STAGE 2

This is the period from 35 to 50 years of age. The main objectives are to make capital gains and create a growing stream of income. Another objective is to develop a diversified portfolio to control the level of risk. Another way to reduce the level of risk is to switch out of the small companies and into medium-size companies that have competitive advantages in established industries. This type of company is found in noncyclical industries such as food products; nondurable household products; medical supplies; personal care products; electric, water, and gas utilities; and waste disposal services. Avoid cyclical businesses like industrial manufacturing, transportation, steel production, residential and commercial construction, travel, and style-based retailing. Companies in these industries have variable earnings and may reduce their dividends during lean times. In addition, their stock prices can decline severely at the bottom of a cycle in the stock market.

Make the transition from small to medium-size companies gradually. If some small companies from Stage 1 have grown into medium size, they can be held if their prospects continue to look promising. Also, any small company whose stock price is ascending at an angle of 20 degrees or higher can be held until the price declines through its 200-day moving average.

STAGE 3

This covers the time span between 50 and 65 years of age. The objective in this period is to maintain a high level of income flow and make some capital gains. The relative safety of each investment is the primary consideration. During this period, companies that are rated AAA, AA, or A by Standard & Poor's rating service are desirable holdings. This keeps risk at a low level. These ratings are available at Web site Quantumonline.com.

During these first three stages, the nine index-based funds that are listed below will be integrated into the suggested bull market portfolios for each five-year period. These funds will be used to facilitate the

Age Group	Specification of Index Content
20 to 25	S&P index of 600 small-cap growth companies
25 to 30	S&P index of 600 small-cap growth and value companies
30 to 35	S&P index of 600 small-cap value companies
35 to 40	S&P index of 400 mid-cap growth companies
40 to 45	S&P index of 400 mid-cap growth and value companies
45 to 50	S&P index of 400 mid-cap value companies
50 to 55	S&P index of 500 large-cap growth companies
55 to 60	S&P index of 500 large-cap growth and value companies
60 to 65	S&P index of 500 large-cap value companies

gradual transition from capital appreciation to capital preservation and from higher risk to lower risk.

STAGE 4

These are the retirement years. After amassing your fortune, the objective is to preserve capital and live on the income from the investments. This requires selling individual common stocks and switching into very low risk assets such as preferred stock issues paying high dividends, real estate investment trust (REIT) funds, and U.S. zero coupon bonds. Your assets must also be protected against inflation. This can be done by holding U.S. Treasury Inflation-Protected Securities (TIPS).

Portfolio Adjustments

During the course of this plan, you will be making many changes in the individual investments you hold. You will make these changes in accord with your personal preferences, desire for capital gains, and tolerance for risk. Here's an overview of how the character of your portfolio will change gradually during the four stages of the portfolio management strategy above.

- From elevated risk to very low or no risk
- From capital gains to capital preservation
- From small-growth stocks to large-value stocks
- From little income to a strong income flow that supports your retirement lifestyle

The plan presented in the following chapters provides detailed guidance for making these transitions smoothly. But while seamless transitions would be ideal, the stock market will present challenges by switching among bull, bear, and range-bound phases. This plan takes these drastically different market phases into consideration by offering separate bull, bear, and range-bound sample portfolios within each five-year period. You will use technical analysis to identify each change in market phase and then adjust your holdings appropriately.

NOTE

The listing of company names in the following chapters does not constitute a recommendation. It is your decision as to whether any particular security is appropriate for your portfolio.

A Historical Perspective

By looking at the history of the stock market, we get some idea of what may lie ahead and why this type of lifetime plan is the best way to prepare for retirement. In the 1930s the Dow Jones Industrial Average reached a low of 200. In 2006 the average reached 12,000, which is a gain of more than 5,000 percent. Based on that potential for appreciation, how much gain might lie in store for the stock market in the next few decades? Using a starting point of 12,000, a gain of 1,000 percent would push the Dow Jones Industrial Average to 120,000. If gains of that magnitude become available, this long-term approach to investing will be an immensely rewarding strategy.

Risk Factors

While the potential rewards of this investment plan are very large, be aware that every investment in the stock market carries an element of risk. The life-spanning strategy takes this factor into consideration by providing investment suggestions that gradually become lower in risk as time passes. The choice of how much risk to take is your decision because you are the only one who knows how much risk you can tolerate. Staying within your comfort zone will help you make appropriate investment decisions.

Risk Level Designations

For each suggested investment presented in the following chapters, a level of risk will be designated in the portfolios. The appropriateness of each level of risk for various types of investors is indicated below.

Risk Level	Appropriate for These Types of Investors
Elevated	Risk-tolerant investors seeking superior capital gains.
Moderate	Investors seeking capital gains equal to those made by the stock market averages.
Low	Investors seeking some capital gains and high income flow.
Very low or none	Risk-averse investors seeking capital preservation with reliable income flow.

Range-Bound or Bear Market?

In the following chapters there will be references to portfolios appropriate for range-bound and bear markets. These portfolios are quite different from each other. Range-bound portfolios emphasize income-producing investments, while the primary objective during a bear market is to preserve capital. It's therefore important to be able to distinguish between these markets as they develop so you can adjust the nature of your investments to achieve these different goals. Here's how you can distinguish between these two market phases as they develop.

To detect the start of a range-bound market, look for the following characteristics. First, there will be mostly moderate daily changes in the Standard & Poor's 500 index and the trading volume will also be moderate. Second, the index will fluctuate above and below its 200-day moving average. Third, the fluctuation of the index will not go more than 15 percent above or below the moving average.

The first indication that a bear market may be starting is a topping pattern taking shape. Another characteristic of the first stage of a bear market is that price moves to the downside become much larger, and they are accompanied by big increases in the trading volume. Price moves to the upside will be short in scope and light on volume. Another sign that a bear market may be starting is that the S&P 500 index goes down through its 200-day moving average. The final confirmation that a bear market is in progress occurs when the index drops 20 percent below its highest point.

NOTE

To estimate the percent of decline in the S&P 500 index, go to Finance.Yahoo.com, enter ^GSPC in the search slot, and click on Get Quotes. Click on Basic Chart in the menu and check the resulting chart. Compare the current price to the highest price shown in the chart and estimate the difference to see if it is more than 20 percent.

Chapter 4

---

*Portfolio Management
for Ages 20 to 25*

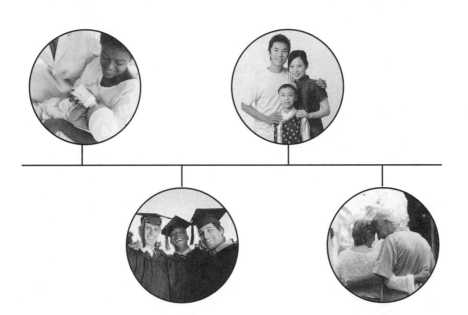

Introduction

As a young person, you are probably not thinking about retirement. But that day will come and if you start preparing for it now, you will be much better off when it arrives. If you have no money to invest at this time, you can begin with a program of self-education. Reading this book will help you understand the basic concept of long-term investing. You can then educate yourself further in the subject areas of most interest to you. Watch informative television programs such as *The Nightly Business Report*. Use the Internet to assist your efforts. Two online sources for basic information are Google and Investopedia.com. These are free services that will give you the answers to any questions you may have about finance and the stock market.

Getting Started

If you have some money to invest, you can start by buying between one and five stocks. If you can only afford to buy one stock, look for one that pays a dividend. Get a newspaper that lists the companies on the New York Stock Exchange. Select a group of companies and write down their names. When you have access to the Internet, use the following procedure to research and evaluate each company.

1. Go to Finance.Yahoo.com.
2. Click on Symbol Lookup.
3. Enter the name of the company in the search slot.
4. Click on Look Up.
5. Check the display that appears.
6. The company symbol appears as one, two, or three letters.
7. Click on the symbol after making a note of it.
8. The Yahoo! Summary display appears.

9. Give preference to companies that are paying a dividend. (The amount and percentage yield appears in the lower right-hand corner.)

10. Make a note of the dividend percentage yield.

11. From the menu of items on the left, select Key Statistics and Competitors.

12. If necessary, refer to Chapter 1 for help with your evaluation of the data on each company.

13. Compare the companies and select the one that has the best qualifications.

14. Check the chart for each company at StockCharts.com to determine the timing of your purchase and refer to Chapter 2 for assistance. (See Charts 2.18 and 2.20.)

NOTE

You will also want to make sure the market is in a bullish uptrend before making your first purchase.

As an alternative to this procedure, a list of stocks that have been pre-qualified are presented in a later section of this chapter, "Potential Investments." If you decide to consider any of those stocks, check the current status at Finance.Yahoo.com.

Information Resources

The *Wall Street Journal* will give you a broad introduction to the world of finance. It reports the latest news on hundreds of companies, provides charts of various market indexes, and prints price quotes on stocks and funds every day. Its detailed, up-to-date reports can help you become familiar with the basic aspects of evaluating a company as a prospect for an investment.

Perhaps you have already been working and saving some of your earnings, and you may have been exploring the Internet for financial information. If so, it is appropriate to start building your portfolio. To do this, buy shares in five companies, each of which is in a different business from the others. This diversifies your stock holdings to give you some control over the level of risk.

Whichever of the above situations you are in, using the information presented in this book will help you get started in the process of accumulating assets. Suggestions about what to purchase will be offered, but the final decisions are yours to make in accord with your personal inclinations.

Guidelines for Investing

Your primary objective in these first years in the stock market is to make large capital gains. Purchasing small-growth stocks is a good way to accomplish this objective. The companies that issue these stocks can be found in young industries where revenue and earnings are growing fast and profit margins are high. These are the characteristics to look for when searching for small companies.

If you are just beginning to invest in the stock market, here are some guidelines to help you get started.

- Don't buy a stock in a downtrend. Wait until the stock price forms a bottom pattern and starts an uptrend before you purchase it.
- Don't open a margin account and borrow money from the broker to buy shares. If the price goes down beyond the limit set by the brokerage, you will have to pay back the loan and you may also lose some of your own money. The most sensible way to make transactions in the stock market is in a cash account.
- Don't enter orders to "Buy at the market." If you do that, you lose control over what you pay for the stock. Instead, place a limit order to buy at a price you specify. That way you, not the

seller, decide how much you pay. If you feel you must own a stock, enter a limit order to buy at the asking price.

- Be wary of advertisements promoting quick trades or day trading. Day trading was very popular for a while and was feasible after the Internet brokers began charging very low commissions. But most of the facilities set up to provide office space for day traders have gone out of business. And most day traders who use their own computers are not able to support themselves in that fashion.

- Don't speculate on stocks listed in the Pink Sheets or the Bulletin Board. These companies do not provide the financial reports required for listing on a major exchange. Because official information is not up to date, they are subject to rumors and misinformation which makes them vulnerable to stock manipulation schemes.

Bull Market Portfolio

This section describes the portfolio contents suggested for the time periods when the market is in an uptrend. There are two components of this portfolio. The first component is a fund that contains a diversified group of small companies that have the potential for making superior capital gains while a bull market is in progress. The vehicle for making this investment is Barclays iShares Standard & Poor's 600 stock fund. This fund tracks the performance of the S&P index of 600 small-capitalization growth stocks.

Barclays investment house is the originator of this type of exchange-traded fund as an investment vehicle and is the largest and most successful manager of these funds. The fund pays a small dividend that covers the annual expense charge of less than 1 percent. The fund is listed on the New York Stock Exchange and trades under the symbol IJT.

Committing 50 percent of your money to this fund and the other 50 percent to one to five small companies of your choosing is an appropriate initial portfolio. To assist your selection process, several small companies that have been increasing their earnings are listed in Chapter 1 in the section titled "Earnings Growth." In the section that follows, four of those companies are presented for your review.

Potential Investments

Hurco Corporation designs and produces computer-controlled machine tools for metalworking companies. It also provides accessories, upgrades, replacement parts, operator training, and software for its machine tool product lines. It sells through distributors and independent agents and it operates in North America, Asia, and Europe. It has an operating profit margin of 15 percent, a P/E ratio of 10, and an annual earnings growth rate of 32 percent. It is one of the most profitable companies in the machine tool industry. The stock ticker symbol is HURC.

Amedisys provides home health care and hospice services. Their services include skilled nursing, physical and occupational therapy, pain management, and psychiatric care. It operates 208 health facilities and 13 hospice agencies in 16 southern states. They have a P/E ratio of 15, an earnings growth rate of 14 percent and an operating profit margin of 10 percent. It is the largest U.S. company in the home health care industry. The stock ticker symbol is AMED.

Encore Wire makes copper electronic wire and cable. It provides wire for houses, apartments, and manufactured housing. It makes cable to conduct power underground as well as for area lighting installations. It provides wire for commercial and industrial buildings. It sells to wholesale distributors and home improvement stores. It has a P/E ratio of 10, an operating profit margin of 17 percent and an earnings growth rate of 20 percent. It is one of the most profitable companies in the industrial electrical equipment industry. The stock ticker symbol is WIRE.

Netflix serves it customers by giving them online access to movie and television show rentals. The customer chooses from among a wide variety of titles. The compact discs are delivered by the Postal Service. Netflix has more than 4 million subscribers. It has a price-to-earnings ratio of 26, an operating profit margin of 5 percent and an earnings growth rate of more than 90 percent. The stock ticker symbol is NFLX.

After performing research to find any additional information desired, you will be in a position to decide if you want to buy any of these companies or look for others instead.

Range-Bound Portfolio

Sometimes the S&P index of 500 stocks fluctuates above and below its moving average and between a support level at the bottom and a resistance level at the top. This situation identifies a range-bound market. (See Chart 4.1.)

This condition can last for a year or much longer. With the market making little or no advance, it's appropriate to switch from the objective of capital gains to the two objectives of high income flow supplemented by some capital gains. One of the best ways to pursue these objectives is through investing in a real estate investment trust (REIT) fund.

Following are four REIT funds for you to consider as a replacement for the Barclays iShares S&P 600 fund during a range-bound market condition. (Indicated dividend rates are subject to change.)

Chart 4.1 Range-Bound Market

- *Cohen & Steers* Advantage Realty Income Fund, symbol RLF. The dividend is approximately 7 percent.
- *AEW Real Estate* Fund, symbol RIF. The dividend is approximately 6.5 percent.
- *ING Clarion Real Estate* Fund, symbol IIA. The dividend is approximately 7.5 percent.
- *HRPT Properties Trust*, symbol HRP. The dividend is approximately 7 percent.

You can get the details on these funds at Finance.Yahoo.com. For a list of additional REIT funds, go to Web site Investinreits.com and click on REIT Mutual Funds.

Bear Market Portfolio

The most challenging problem for investors occurs when a bear market is imminent. When the S&P 500 index declines through its 200-day moving average, it may indicate the start of a bear market. (See Chart 4.2.) The other possibility is that the market becomes range-bound. The challenge is to make a decision in a timely fashion without rushing to act or delaying too long. To help in this situation, here is a procedure to use.

Go to Finance.Yahoo.com. Enter their symbol for the S&P 500 index (^GSPC) in the search slot and click GO. Select Technical Analysis from the menu on the left side of the screen. From the row of mov-

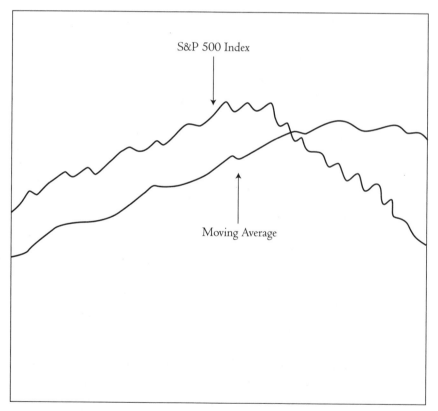

Chart 4.2 Bear Market Starts

ing averages, select 200. Scroll down to see the chart you have requested. Note the relationship between the S&P 500 index and its 200-day moving average. If the index has been consistently above its average and it drops through it, either a bear market or a range-bound market is coming. It is more likely to be a bear market if the preceding bull market rise has been at a very high angle of ascent or has been parabolic. (See Charts 4.3 and 4.4.) It is more likely to be a range-bound market if the preceding rise has been at an angle of ascent less than 45 degrees.

NOTE

If there is any problem with the Web site, here is an alternative procedure. Go to StockCharts.com. Press the drop down menu icon and

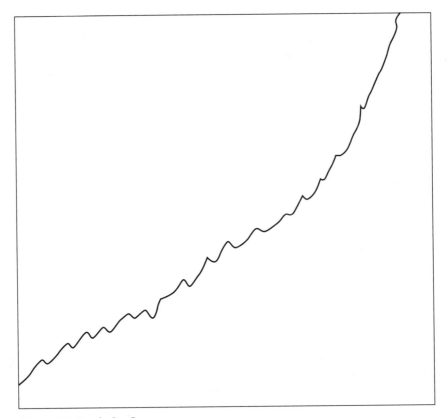

Chart 4.3 Parabolic Curve

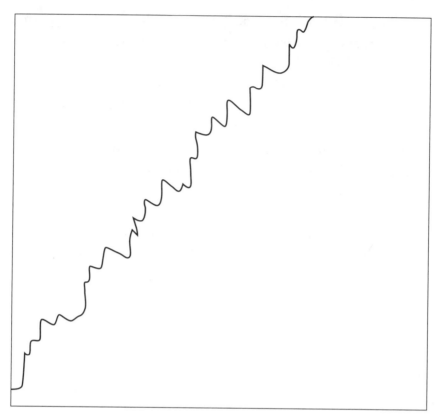

Chart 4.4 High Angle of Ascent

select Gallery View. Enter their symbol, $SPX, in the search slot and click Go. Check the chart labeled Daily View. See if the S&P 500 index is dropping through the 200-day moving average. If so, check this situation frequently until you can decide which type of market will develop.

Here is a way to make an educated guess as to the duration of a bear market. If a preceding bull market ended in a parabolic curve or an uptrend with a high angle of ascent, there is a likelihood the bear market will be short. In this situation, sell your stocks and the fund and put your cash in the brokerage's money market account to preserve your gains.

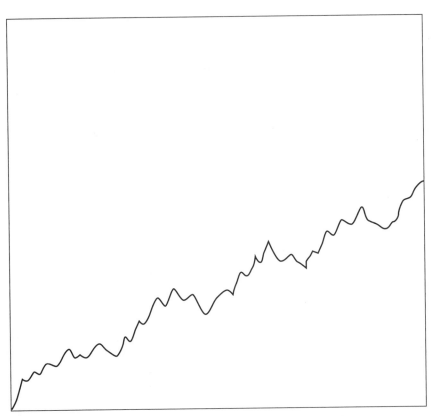

Chart 4.5 Moderate Angle of Ascent

On the other hand, if the preceding advance in the market average was at an angle of ascent of 45 degrees or less, it is more likely the bear market decline will be gradual and last at least a year. See Chart 4.5.

Zero Coupon Bonds

In this situation put 80 percent of your money into one-year U.S. zero coupon bonds. (Each bond has a par value of $1,000 but is sold at a discount from that price. The discount amount depends on the interest rate at the time of purchase.) Zero coupon bonds can be bought through your broker or your bank or directly from the U.S. government at their Web site, treasurydirect.gov.

Money Market Accounts

Place the remaining 20 percent in a money market account the brokerage maintains to have some cash readily available. This is a safe place to keep the funds when stock prices are declining. While waiting for the next bull market, conduct research to decide which stocks to buy when the bear market is over.

As the new bull market begins to establish an uptrend, sell the zero coupon bonds. You can then purchase the individual stocks you have been researching and also repurchase shares in the Barclays iShares S&P 600 index tracking fund, symbol IJT.

Suggested Portfolio Contents

The following are portfolio suggestions for the three types of markets: bull, range-bound, and bear. You need growth-type investments to take advantage of a rising bull market, a balance between capital gains and high income to prosper in a range-bound market, and riskless bonds and a money market account to preserve your assets in a bear market.

	Bull Market
Objective	Superior capital gains
Risk Levels	Elevated for individual stocks; low for fund.
Suggestions	Barclays fund that tracks the S&P 600 index (IJT), 50 percent
	1 to 5 small-cap growth stocks, each in a different industry, 50 percent
	Range-Bound Market
Objectives	High income with some capital gains
Risk Levels	Elevated for individual stocks; low for REIT fund

| Suggestions | REIT fund, 50 percent |
| | 1 to 5 small-cap growth stocks, each in a different industry, 50 percent |

Bear Market

Objective	Preserve capital
Risk Levels	Very low for money market fund; no risk for zero coupon bonds
Suggestions	Money market fund, 20 percent
	U.S. zero coupon bonds, 80 percent
	Or
	Money market fund, 100 percent if you feel the bear market will be short.

Chapter 5

Portfolio Management for Ages 25 to 30

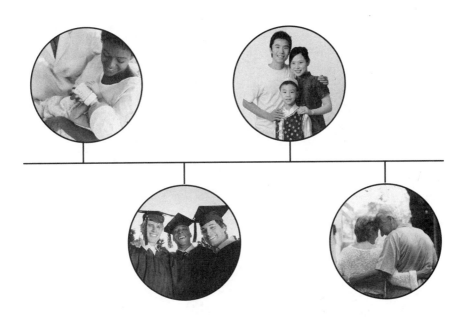

Introduction

Your primary objective in these years is to make large capital gains by owning stock in small companies with growth potential. These companies are in young industries where revenue and earnings are increasing fast and profit margins are high. This chapter contains some suggestions to help you find these companies.

Becoming skillful at picking winning stocks will depend on how well you learn to use the basic concepts of fundamental and technical analysis. It will also be directly proportional to how much time and effort you are willing to spend doing research before buying a stock. Here are some questions and suggestions to help you evaluate and improve your investing practices.

Performance Review

Have you bought a stock that was declining in price and then watched it go much lower? Some investors believe a stock that has dropped a long distance is a bargain. Unfortunately, once downward momentum becomes established, it often continues longer than most investors expect. Hopefully your answer to the preceding question is "No," and you will resist the temptation to buy stocks that are in downtrends.

Do you have a margin account? Have you ever borrowed money from your broker to buy a stock? Have you ever had a margin call from your broker to put up more money because your stock went down too far? Has your broker ever sold a stock you had on margin because it went down beyond the limit established by the brokerage? If you answered "No" to those questions because you have a cash account, you have chosen a sensible method for transacting business in the stock market. If you answered "Yes" to any of those questions and you want to prevent unpleasant collection calls from your broker, convert your margin account into a cash account.

Do you tell your broker to buy or sell for you without specifying the price by a limit order? If you are allowing your broker or the other party to the transaction to determine the price, you are trading from a disadvantageous position. When you set the price you are willing to pay to buy, or to receive when you sell, you are representing your interest in an effective manner. On the other hand, when you buy or sell "at the market" you are relinquishing your right to get favorable prices. Over the long run, this will increase your cost of making transactions by a large amount. Assert your right to get better prices by using limit orders in your transactions.

Have you ever bought call or put options? Did you make any profits on them? If so, you are either very lucky or a very sophisticated trader. The dismaying fact is that 80 percent of options expire unexercised and the purchase price is lost. The reason for this high percentage is that there are three ways a buyer of options can lose.

1. The price goes in the right direction, but it doesn't go far enough.
2. The price goes in the wrong direction.
3. There is very little price movement and the time limit expires.

So the odds are stacked three to one against the buyers of calls and puts.

The argument for buying options is that the buyer puts up a small sum for the chance of making a large gain, and the potential loss is limited. The reason most options expire unexercised is because time runs out before it is profitable to exercise them. Therefore the basic problem facing the buyer is that options are a wasting asset. Investors who follow the lifetime investment plan recommended in this book will have much better results than those who trade options.

Bull Market Portfolio

There are two components of this bull market portfolio. Half of the assets should be invested in a fund that tracks the performance of S&P index of 600 small-cap stocks. The vehicle for making this investment is a Barclays fund that includes a blend of growth and value stocks. The value component of the fund provides a lower degree of risk than is contained in an all-growth stock fund. This fund pays a dividend that covers the small annual expense charge. The fund is listed on the New York Stock Exchange and trades under the symbol IJR.

The second half of your assets should be invested in five small-capitalization growth stocks, each of which is in an industry different from the others. This variety produces a diverse group which keeps the risk level moderate. To assist your selection process, several small companies that have been increasing their earnings are listed in Chapter I in the section titled, "Earnings Growth." In the following section two of those companies are presented for your consideration.

Potential Investments

Wayside Technology (WSTG) sells software, hardware, and support services for microcomputers, servers, and networks to corporations, government agencies, and educational institutions. It also sells technical software to corporate resellers, consultants, and systems integrators. It has offices in the United States and Canada. It has no debt, a P/E ratio of 18, and an earnings growth rate over 50 percent.

VASCO Data Security (VDSI) designs and markets hardware and software security systems worldwide. It has patented products for business and commercial enterprises which enable secure financial transactions over the Internet and private networks. It has an earnings growth rate of 60 percent, an operating profit margin of 20 percent and a P/E ratio of 35.

NOTE

See Chapter 4 for descriptions of the operations and data on four more companies.

Earning growth rates and P/E ratios are subject to change.

Stock Performance Evaluation

After you select and purchase the companies you want, your initial portfolio for a bull market in this five-year time period will be complete. It is most likely, however, that one or more of the stocks purchased will not live up to your expectations. Staying aware of the performance of these investments is an important part of portfolio management. At least once a week, review the status of each stock. This can be done by going to StockCharts.com. Press the drop down menu icon and select Gallery View. Enter a stock symbol in the search slot and click Go. A daily chart appears which shows the stock price and its 200-day moving average. Scroll down to see a weekly chart. If the price of the stock has gone down through the moving average the stock should be sold.

NOTE

Internet Web sites are subject to change. If you can't find an item by following the suggested procedure, explore the site until you discover the sequence that will provide the desired result, or see Appendix C for additional helpful Web sites.

Range-Bound Portfolio

A bull market may end before this five-year period is finished. It is important to detect a change in the phase of the market as it occurs. Either a range-bound or a bear market may come after the bull market ends.

When the S&P index of 500 stocks fluctuates above and below its 200-day moving average and within resistance and support levels, it indicates a range-bound market has arrived. (See Chart 4.1.) Since the upward momentum of the market may be lost for a year and longer, switch from the single objective of large capital gains to the dual objectives of capital gains and high income flow.

Sell the poorly performing stocks and the Barclays fund that tracks the performance of the S&P 600 index of small stocks. With the proceeds from these sales, make another investment which can provide a high income flow along with the possibility for some capital gain. This new investment is a real estate investment trust fund. This type of fund is required to pay its shareholders dividends totaling 90 percent of its net income. Dividends are paid monthly and are reliable because the fund gets its revenue and income from rental fees collected from a wide variety of business and residential properties. Here are three funds for you to review. Select one to replace the Barclays fund.

- RMR Real Estate Fund (RMR). The dividend is approximately 6.8 percent, and it is paid monthly.
- Cohen & Steers Premium Income Fund (RPF). The dividend is approximately 6.5 percent, and it is paid monthly.
- Neuberger Berman Real Estate Income Fund (NRO). The dividend is approximately 6.4 percent, and it is paid monthly.

You can get details on these funds at Finance.Yahoo.com home page and by clicking on menu items Profile and Key Statistics. Also, click on Technical Analysis and then on the 200-day moving average. Evaluate the performance of the fund. For a list of more real estate investment trust funds, go to Investinreits.com and click on REIT Mutual Funds.

NOTE

Dividend rates are subject to change. To get the current rate, check the summary display at Finance.Yahoo.com.

Bear Market Portfolio

If the S&P 500 index declines through its 200-day moving average and goes into a downtrend, it may indicate a bear market is beginning. To check on this possibility, go to StockCharts.com. At the top of the page Sharp Charts appears. Insert $SPX in the search slot and click Go. The day-by-day record of the S&P 500 index and its 200-day moving average appears in red. Review the relationship between the index and its 200-day moving average to see if a bear market may be starting.

Bear markets last from several months to a couple of years. The average duration is approximately 14 months. To deal with a bear market effectively, there are some actions you should take. Sell your stocks and the fund and place the proceeds in your brokerage's money market account. Then make an estimate of how long the bear market will last. To do this, go to the Web site Moneycentral.msn.com. Click on Investing, then enter the symbol $INX and click on 2 y to check the two-year history of the S&P 500 index prior to the beginning of the bear market. If the index had been rising sharply in a parabolic curve or at an angle of ascent greater than 45 degrees, the bear market is likely to end quickly. (See Charts 4.3 and 4.4.) The likelihood of a fast ending is increased if the decline is steep and the trading volume is at very high levels.

However, if the advance in the S&P 500 index was at an angle of ascent less than 45 degrees, it is likely the bear market will last longer than a year. The chance the bear market will be long lived is higher if the decline is gradual and the trading volume is at average levels or below.

If it appears the bear market will be short lived, keep your cash in the money market account and collect the interest until a new bull market begins. If a long-lived bear market appears to be likely, use your money market cash to buy one-year U.S. zero coupon bonds. When they mature, reinvest the money into three-month bonds and continue that procedure until the bear market ends. In the meantime, review the trading activity of the market frequently to be aware of any bottoming pattern. When the new bull market begins, sell the zero coupon bonds. Use half of the proceeds to buy back into the Barclays fund. Use the other half to buy five small-capitalization growth stocks. Refer to Chapter 1 to find candidates for these purchases.

If you can't find worthwhile candidates there, review a copy of the *Investor's Business Daily* Monday edition. In the second section you will see a list of 100 selected stocks, each of which is accompanied by a small chart showing the stock prices and a moving average. Look for companies whose stock charts show rising moving averages. Make a list of those you like and go to Finance.Yahoo.com and check the fundamental condition of each company as described in Chapter 1. Also go to StockCharts.com and check the technical condition of each company's stock price as described in Chapter 2.

Suggested Portfolio Contents

The following summary shows the portfolios for the three phases of the market. The portfolios evolve from risk tolerant in the bull phase to income seeking with moderate risk in the range-bound phase and from there to risk-averse preservation of capital in the bear phase.

Bull Market	
Objective	Superior capital gains
Risk Levels	Elevated for individual stocks; low for fund
Suggestions	5 small-cap stocks, 50 percent
	Barclays S&P 600 fund, IJR, 50 percent
Range-Bound Market	
Objectives	High income with some capital gains
Risk Levels	Moderate for individual stocks; low for fund

| Suggestions | 5 small-cap stocks, 50 percent |
| | REIT income fund, 50 percent |

Bear Market

Objectives	Preserve capital and receive income
Risk Levels	None for bonds; very low for money market fund
Suggestions	Money market fund, 100 percent for short bear market
	or
	Zero coupon bonds, 100 percent for long bear market

Chapter 6

Portfolio Management for Ages 30 to 35

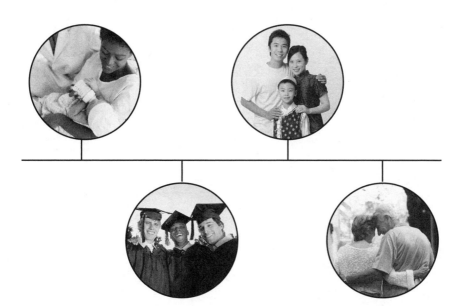

Introduction

As an investor in your thirties, you have probably been through both a bull and bear market. If so, you are well aware of the challenges of investing in stocks. Riding a financial roller coaster can be just as stomach churning as the vertical drops of the coasters in the amusement parks. Hopefully you have learned that investing successfully requires fortitude, patience, flexibility, and a willingness to do research before putting money at risk.

The stock market can be very rewarding for those who treat it with respect, but it can be very punishing to those who regard it as a gambling casino. It is not the place to speculate on long shots. What it does offer is the means to reach your financial goal if you are willing to make a sustained effort. To help you in your quest, this book provides information, research procedures, a life-spanning approach, and some investment suggestions to guide you along the way.

In the years between the ages of 20 and 35, the primary objective is to make large capital gains through the vehicle of small stocks with growth potential. It's also important to find stocks that pay dividends and increase those payments as the years go by. This chapter contains some suggestions to help in your search to find those companies and capture both capital gains and significant income flow.

Bull Market Portfolio

In Chapter 1 there is a list of companies that have a competitive advantage. This list is located in the section titled, "Competitive Situation." To start creating your portfolio for the next bull market, review that list and select 10 companies. Look for companies that are leaders in their industries. As you pick the companies you want to research, select only one company from a particular industry. This way you have a diversified group to keep the risk level down. Here is the research procedure to follow. Write down the stock symbols for 10 or more of the companies in your list. Go to Finance.Yahoo.com and enter each symbol in the search slot. When the summary display comes up, look in the lower right-hand corner and write down the dividend yield percentage.

If there is no dividend indicated, reject that company. After you have 10 companies on your list, enter a company symbol in the search slot and click on the menu item Competitors. On the page that appears, check the following items: Market Cap, Quarterly Rev. Growth, and Operating Margin. Make an assessment of how much advantage the company has over its competitors in each of these categories. If it appears to be ahead of the other companies in the industry, put it on your list of potential purchases.

The next step is to evaluate the technical condition of each company's stock price pattern. Go to StockCharts.com. Press the drop down menu icon and select Gallery View. Enter the company's symbol in the search slot and click Go. Check the daily chart. Here's how to evaluate the technical relationship between the stock price and its moving average. First, the stock price should be above the 200-day moving average. Next, the moving average should be slanting upward. Estimate the angle of ascent or measure it with a protractor. Record the angle on the list next to the name of the company. Angles between 20 and 30 degrees are desirable as they are sustainable and can produce sizeable gains. Next, make sure the stock price is not making a topping pattern. Finally, give the stock price and moving average relationship a rating of acceptable, good, or excellent and notate the rating on the list. After completing this process and buying the 10 companies with the top ratings, you will have a diversified group of strong competitors that pays dividends. Invest about 50 percent of your portfolio in these companies.

Monitoring Your Portfolio

After you have purchased the stocks, it's helpful to have a convenient way to monitor their progress. An Internet brokerage provides a means for doing this. Use their service to set up a portfolio that will be automatically updated. Establish the portfolio by entering the symbol for each stock, the purchase price, the number of shares purchased, and the commission cost. If the service does not enter the total cost of the purchase automatically, enter it yourself. This allows you to compare the current value of the purchase against the original cost and see the gain or loss.

Once you have the 10 stocks listed, you will be able to check on the progress for each stock and for the entire portfolio as frequently as you want. This setup will give you the capability to compare each stock against the others. When you spot a stock that is lagging behind, you can go to Finance.Yahoo.com and check the relationship between the stock price and its 200-day moving average. By staying abreast of this condition, you will be able to decide when a stock should be sold. After selling a stock, you would then use the selection procedure described above to find a replacement.

Barclays Index Tracking Fund

The other half of the portfolio should consist of the Barclays fund which tracks the S&P index of 600 small companies selected for value. The symbol for this fund is IJS. Monitor the performance of the S&P index of 500 stocks until you see a bottom formation that marks the beginning of a bull market. The symbol is ^GSPC on the Finance.Yahoo.com Web site. The time to buy the Barclays fund is when the uptrend becomes established.

NOTE

As you invest in these two parts of your portfolio, you may want to change the portions that go into each part from the 50/50 basis to emphasize one part or the other. If you do that, be aware that increasing the amount invested in the individual stocks raises both the potential for capital gains and the level of risk.

While you are waiting for a bull market to begin, check to see if the market is in a range-bound phase. You can do this by observing the action of the S&P index of 500 stocks; symbol ^GSPC. Go to Finance.Yahoo.com, enter the symbol, click on the menu item Technical Analysis and select the 200-day moving average on the next screen. Scroll down to check the chart you have created. If the index is confined within support and resistance levels, a range-bound market condition exists and a different portfolio mix is appropriate as explained in the following section.

Range-Bound Portfolio

A bull market portfolio focuses on getting large capital gains. A range-bound portfolio is more appropriately oriented toward increasing income flow. If the market stays within the range for an extended time period, there will be less opportunity for capital gains. That's the reason for adding an investment that pays high dividends during this time period. A good place to get this high yield is from real estate investment trust funds (REITs). These funds are required to pay 90 percent of their net income to their stockholders. Since the income received by REITs is derived from rent receipts, their earnings are reliable and many of these funds pay dividends once a month.

In the years ahead, REIT funds will play a major role in generating income to enrich your portfolio during range-bound market phases. For this reason it's appropriate for you to know about the types of investments you hold when you purchase a REIT fund. Below is a list of these funds, along with the types of real property assets each fund holds.

NOTE

Dividend rates are subject to change.

REIT Fund Properties

AIM Select Real Estate fund (RRE) owns the following types of real properties: health care facilities, office buildings, industrial parks, apartment buildings, self-storage facilities, hotel resorts, and specialized facilities. This fund provides a dividend of approximately 8 percent.

Nuveen Real Estate fund (JRS) has ownership of health care facilities, hotels and resorts, industrial parks, office buildings, regional malls, shopping centers, and self-storage facilities. This fund provides a dividend of approximately 7.5 percent.

Cohen & Steers Total Return fund (RFI) owns health care facilities, apartment buildings, shopping centers, office complexes, industrial parks, and hotels. This fund provides a dividend of approximately 6 percent.

ING Clarion Global Real Estate (IGR) has regional malls, multipurpose buildings, shopping centers, warehouses, apartment buildings, and specialty structures. This fund gives a dividend of approximately 6.5 percent.

Real Estate Income (RIT) has holdings in office buildings, apartment buildings, health care facilities, industrial parks, hotels and resorts, regional malls, and shopping centers. This fund provides a dividend of 6.5 percent.

Neuberger Berman Realty Income fund (NRI) has apartment buildings, commercial buildings, health care facilities, hotels, industrial parks, office buildings, and self-storage facilities. This fund has a dividend of 6.5 percent.

If you see a range-bound market phase developing, sell the Barclays iShares Standard & Poor's 600 fund. You can then purchase one or more REIT funds as part of the investments you will hold during the range-bound market. Continue holding any individual stocks that are in uptrends of 20 degrees or higher.

Bear Market Portfolio

Unfortunately at times, bear markets develop, and they provide a temporary delay in the process of acquiring capital gains. The most obvious sign a bear market has begun is the downward penetration of the S&P index of 500 stocks through its 200-day moving average. A warning sign is the formation of one of the topping patterns illustrated in Chapter 2. When you see these signs, it's time to sell the investments you had in a preceding bull or range-bound phase. Put the proceeds into your brokerage's money market fund. Or you can invest that money in U.S. zero coupon bonds.

Suggested Portfolio Contents

The following section contains a summary of the investments suggested for the three phases of the market described in this chapter. This summary can serve as a reference on how to manage your portfolio as the market transitions from phase to phase.

	Bull Market
Objective	Superior capital gains with some income
Risk Levels	Moderate for individual stocks; low for small-cap fund
Suggestions	10 small-cap stocks, 50 percent
	Barclays tracking fund of S&P index of 600 small-cap value stocks (IJS), 50 percent

Range-Bound Market

Objectives	High income with some capital gains
Risk Levels	Moderate for individual stocks; low for REIT funds
Suggestions	Individual stocks in uptrends of 20 degrees or higher, 50 percent
	REIT funds paying high dividends, 50 percent

Bear Market

Objectives	Preserve capital and receive some income
Risk Levels	Very low for brokerage's money market fund; no risk for zero coupon bonds
Suggestions	Money market funds, 100 percent
	or
	Zero coupon bonds, 100 percent (Choose the higher rate of return.)

Chapter 7

*Portfolio Management
for Ages 35 to 40*

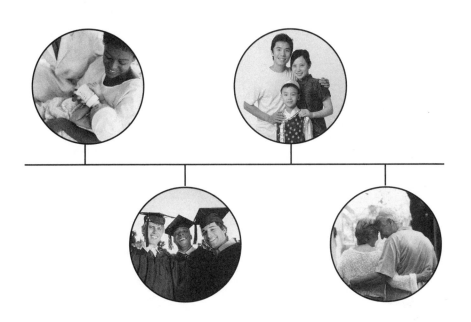

Introduction

During these five years, a continuing effort to capture capital gains and build income flow is required. These are the basic elements of a wealth-building investment strategy. Another important component of the strategy is the ability to recognize the bull and bear phases of the market. By noting the switch between these market conditions and making the necessary changes to your portfolio, you will maximize the growth of your assets over the long term. The following sections provide an analysis of market movements to help you recognize those two volatile market phases so you can profit from the uptrend and avoid losses in the downtrend.

Analyzing Market Phases

Bull markets are the most accommodative in support of achieving large capital gains. It's therefore critical to your success to become familiar with their characteristics. Bull markets usually last several years. They start out slowly and build momentum as they proceed. In the beginning, a bull market usually has an angle of ascent between 10 and 30 degrees as shown by its 200-day moving average. In the middle phase, the angle increases to between 30 and 45 degrees. In the final phase the ascent usually has a rate in excess of 45 degrees or it exhibits a parabolic curve. See Charts 4.3 and 4.4.

During both of these end stages, many investors are very happy with their capital gains and the stock market is a frequent topic of discussion at social gatherings. Anchorpersons on business television shows play the role of cheerleaders for the stock market. Business magazines print positive articles about the market, and the most successful companies are highlighted on the covers.

In the market the volume of trading is very large, as price records are broken by the market averages. People who have made huge capital gains pass stock tips to their friends and associates and talk about their successful trades. These levels of success breed arrogance, and speculators purchase stocks with excessively high price-to-earnings ratios. Speculators begin to feel euphoric. Finally, when most of the available cash has been committed, a market top forms. As the top is being completed, the market index drops through its 200-day moving average and a bear market begins.

Bear Market Characteristics

As the bear market goes into the initial stages of decline, many investors are not convinced the bull market is over. They believe the decline will reverse itself, and prices will go up again. So they hold on to their stocks in a condition psychologists might label "denial," which is the refusal to see something that is obvious.

As the downward momentum builds, disbelieving investors watch their paper profits disappearing quickly. Those investors who were caught off guard by the decline experience feelings of doubt and depression. These feelings grow into panic as prices continue to erode. Eventually the masses of market participants sell out their holdings because they can't stand the pain anymore. This selling has been labeled "capitulation," and it marks the end of the bear market.

Controlling Emotions

How can investors avoid being caught up in these kinds of emotional reactions? Investors who are overwhelmed by their emotions are those who don't have a logic-based investment strategy to help them get through the market swings. By following the long-term approach outlined in this book you can avoid the emotional reactions which can be so damaging to your prospects for success.

The critical element in having a logical strategy is to use technical analysis to identify the tops and bottoms as the market swings between its bull and bear phases. Chapter 2 provides illustrations of the price patterns that identify the changes in the direction of the market. After the market has been going up or down for an extended period, it is prudent to check frequently for the price patterns in the market averages that indicate the possible end of that market phase. Using technical analysis to determine when to buy or sell rather than relying on your hopes and fears is one of the keys to investment success.

Independent Research

Another key to investing successfully over the long term is to do independent research so you can find opportunities most other investors are not aware of because they have not been publicized by the investment community. These undiscovered stocks trade at bargain prices because their growth potential has not been recognized and a strong demand for them has yet to develop. Finding such stocks before others do requires doing your own research. This chapter provides guidelines for discovering these stocks so you can add them to your portfolio.

Research Project

Barron's weekly magazine lists all of the stocks traded on the National Association of Securities Dealers Automated Quotations (Nasdaq) market. Many well-known large companies are listed there, but there are also many lesser-known medium-sized companies in the list. The heading over the list is labeled "Nasdaq Issues." This is a good place to start looking for unpublicized, growing companies. Here is a recommended procedure to follow in conducting this research.

Look for unfamiliar names. Note that the stock ticker symbol is shown after each name. Under the column headings of "Weeks" and "Last," the closing price of the preceding Friday appears. Look for stock prices in the range of $5 to $20. Record the name, symbol, and closing price for each company's stock of interest to you. Next, check the figures under the columns with the headings of "Earnings" and "Latest Year," "This Year," and "Next Year." If there are negative numbers in the last two columns, exclude that company from your list. Don't include any company where the figure in the last column is lower than the one in the preceding column. The companies to put on your list are the ones where the positive number in the last column is a large percentage higher than the one in the preceding column. For example

Latest year = .20   This year = .30   Next year = .50

Create a list of 10 to 20 companies that are currently paying dividends and for which an increase in earnings is projected.

Technical Analysis

For the next phase of this research project, go to StockCharts.com. Click on the drop down menu icon and select "Gallery View." Enter each symbol into the search slot. A daily chart appears first and by scrolling down, a weekly chart is revealed. The daily chart has a 200-day moving average and the weekly chart has a 40-week moving average, the same length in business days. Check the relationship between the stock price and its moving average. The stock price should be above the average, which should be rising at an angle of 20 degrees or more. Another acceptable pattern is a price that has crossed up through the moving average. If you decide the price and moving average patterns are positive, make a record of the name of the company and its stock symbol.

NOTE

Internet Web sites are subject to change. If you can't find the item you want by following the specified procedure, explore the site until you find what you are looking for. Or refer to Appendix C where you will find additional helpful Web sites.

Fundamental Analysis

After writing your assessment of the technical condition of the stock price chart, you are ready to start on the fundamental analysis portion of the evaluation. Go to Finance.Yahoo.com, enter the ticker symbol of the company you're researching, and click on the menu item "Key Statistics." In this display, review these items and look for the following characteristics.

- The operating profit margin should be at least 10 percent.
- The year-over-year percentage gain must be positive and the higher, the better.
- Little or no debt is a positive factor.
- Cash flow must be positive and the higher, the better.
- If the trailing P/E is higher than 30, the forward P/E should be 20 or lower.

Next, click on the item "Competitors" in the menu. Check to see how the company compares to the others in the display. The desirable situation is for the company to have large advantages over the others. If the superiority is relatively minor, that is also acceptable. But if the company is operating at a lower level than the others, that is disqualifying. If your evaluation of the company's overall fundamental qualifications is positive, enter it in your notes as a candidate for your portfolio.

The final part of the review is to look at the bottom of this display of competitors and note which industry the company is in. To ensure a diversified portfolio, do not have more than one company per industry. After completing this review and ensuring there is no industry duplication, you will know which companies can be included in your portfolio.

Bull Market Portfolio

Your portfolio in this five-year time period will include the 10 undiscovered companies you selected from *Barron's* magazine. This segment of your portfolio should produce superior capital gains during a bull market. The other half of your portfolio will be the Barclays fund that tracks the performance of the S&P 400 index of medium-sized stocks with growth potential. This fund, which has the ticker symbol IJK, provides diversification and a lower level of risk than the individual stocks.

Range-Bound Portfolio

If the market becomes range-bound during this five-year period, it will be necessary to change the content of your portfolio to compensate for the lack of advance. With the market averages fluctuating aimlessly, the Barclays fund of 400 medium-sized stocks will not produce positive results. Replace it with a real estate investment trust (REIT) fund that pays a large dividend. A listing of REIT funds, along with their dividend rates, is provided in Chapter 6 in the section titled, "REIT Fund Properties." In addition to providing a large income stream, these funds may also produce capital gains because of their property holdings.

Some of the individual company stocks you discovered for your bull market portfolio can continue to be held during a range-bound market if they are providing capital gains. You should compare the results these stocks produce to determine which ones are doing the best. Then sell the poorest performers and find some more undiscovered companies to complete your portfolio for the range-bound market.

Bear Market Portfolio

As soon as you decide the market going into a bearish phase, take action to preserve your assets by selling the individual stocks and the Barclays fund. If the market has been range-bound, you would sell the REIT fund. In either case it would be necessary to move the proceeds into the brokerage's money market fund, because diversification doesn't protect against losses when there is a broad decline in equities as occurs in a bear market.

You may leave your cash in the money market fund until the bear market ends. Or you may buy U.S. zero coupon bonds if they provide a better return on investment than the fund. Your broker will let you know which return is higher. If you buy the zero coupon bonds, you can sell them before they mature as soon as you see the bear market is over.

Suggested Portfolio Contents

A summary of the three portfolios is shown below for your reference. It indicates how selections of investments support your objectives as they change from one market phase to another.

NOTE

For a description of how to distinguish between the start of range-bound and bear markets, see the last section of Chapter 3.

	Bull Market
Objectives	Superior capital gains and dividend income
Risk Levels	Moderate for individual stocks; low for fund
Suggestions	Ten undiscovered companies, 50 percent
	Barclays S&P 400 tracking fund, IJK, 50 percent

Range-Bound Market	
Objectives	Income from dividends and some capital gains
Risk Levels	Moderate for individual stocks; low for fund
Suggestions	Ten undiscovered companies, 50 percent
	REIT fund paying high dividends, 50 percent

Bear Market	
Objective	Preserve capital
Risk Levels	Very low for money market fund
	None for U.S. zero coupon bonds
Suggestions	Brokerage's money market fund, 100 percent
	or
	U.S. zero coupon bonds 100 percent

Chapter 8

A Broader Perspective

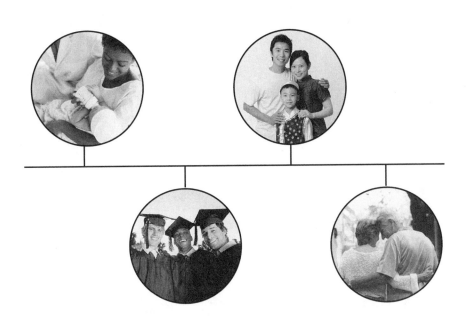

Introduction

You are now at the midpoint of this lifetime plan. Previously the focus has been on the specifics of portfolio development and management. But there are some aspects of successful investing that are broader than those activities. Let's begin with a personal factor that can produce high-quality results.

An Independent Mind

One of the most important assets an investor can have is the ability to think independently. In a world based on being connected, you are subjected to many attempts to influence your decisions. These intrusions on your thoughts may not be in your best interest. Friends and associates offer stock tips; your broker may encourage you to trade too often; guests on financial TV shows offer many recommendations; and Internet Web sites and business magazines push "hot" stocks.

If you act on those suggestions, you are putting your trust where it is not deserved. The reason those tips have little value is that you are the one who knows what is in your best interest. You know your financial condition, needs, objectives, and level of risk tolerance. Your investments should reflect this personal knowledge and should be based on your own independent research.

Conflicts of Interest

If you are making all or some of your stock market transactions through a traditional brokerage, the broker's interest is usually quite different from yours. The broker may be friendly, knowledgeable, and helpful, but he or she is basically a salesperson. This means that his or her objective is to make sales to you and other customers in order to earn commissions. The conflict of interest occurs in several ways.

First, the more transactions you make, the larger are the commissions. Second, the highest commissions for a transaction occur when the broker sells you an investment that is sponsored by the brokerage. This is because brokerage management offers the broker an extra incentive to sell from their inventory. When the broker is successful in getting you to buy directly out of the brokerage's holdings, that sale works to the benefit of the broker and the brokerage, but it may not be the best investment for you.

Third, another conflict of interest may develop when the broker recommends that you buy shares in a fund. Mutual funds vary with reference to content, fees, commissions, front- or back-end loading, tax liabilities, etc. The broker is likely to sell you the fund that provides the highest commission or other compensation. But again, the fund the broker wants to sell may not be the best one for you to buy.

The general situation is that the investment community conducts a continuous promotional effort to convince you to buy its products and services. When you make a purchase based solely on their recommendation, you are trusting a self-serving operation.

Research Aids

The Internet is a convenient place to conduct research. We have been referring to StockCharts.com and Finance.Yahoo.com because they are the best sites for technical and fundamental information. There are several other helpful sites which are described in Appendix C.

There is also a lot of information in the print media. *Barron's* weekly magazine gives detailed reports of the latest news on companies listed on the exchanges, reviews all the mutual and closed-end funds; outlines the prospects for individual companies; reports buy and sell transactions by company officials; presents stock price charts; lists prices for all stocks on the major exchanges; projects earnings for each company for the current year and for next year; and provides current price information on preferred stocks and U.S. government bonds. *Barron's* is available at some newsstands, in stores, and in many public libraries.

Investor's Business Daily is a respected publisher of financial news. It has special features on business leaders, Internet and technology companies, health care and medical companies, and trends in selected industries. In the Monday edition, it gives financial data on the 20 top-performing stocks during the preceding week. It also shows the prices with their moving averages for 100 stocks. This is an excellent source for finding stocks with strong upward momentum.

The *Wall Street Journal* is the most widely read newspaper covering the business world. It is distributed nationwide and internationally. It publishes the latest in-depth news on several companies every business day. It lists all the transactions on the New York, American, and Nasdaq exchanges. It reports the trading activities of exchange traded funds. In its "Marketplace" section it covers developments in technology, health care, media, and marketing.

BusinessWeek magazine provides a wealth of information on many companies. It has special features on global businesses, information technology, scientific advances, and the outlook for the economy. It has frequent articles on topics such as the best companies for earnings growth and those having the highest recognition worldwide. And it publishes reports on investments that have been overlooked by Wall Street analysts.

Television versus Investors

There are a number of television shows that encourage speculation in the stock market. In the course of a week, hundreds of stocks are recommended for purchase. Some investors enter buy orders immediately if the market is open. This is not a sensible way to make investment decisions. First, the price of the stock will usually be inflated quickly as the rush to buy it develops. Second, the person making the recommendation may own the stock and may be trying to push the stock price higher for his or her own benefit. Third, some commentators recommend a stock be bought, while others say it should be sold. How can you know which side is right? Following the recommendations of guests on TV programs is not a prudent way to make investments. These television shows should be regarded as entertainment rather than as a place to get reliable information on companies and their stocks.

Television for Investors

On a more positive note, if you rise early and want to have current business information to start your day, there are two shows available. Starting at 5:00 A.M. Eastern time, CNBC has a show called *Worldwide Exchange*, which has anchors in New York, London, and Singapore to provide business news from the United States, Europe, and Asia. CNBC broadcasts throughout the business day.

Starting at 5:00 A.M. Eastern time, *Bloomberg Television* also provides business news. It has a ticker tape showing prices for a selected group of U.S. based company stocks trading in Europe. It also provides comprehensive coverage of business news on a global basis. This show lasts until 8:00 A.M. Eastern time.

Internet Brokerages

If you are now making your transactions through a traditional brokerage, it would be to your advantage to also have an account with an Internet broker. With your ability to generate your own investment ideas, you would be able to take advantage of the lower commissions charged by the Internet brokerages. You would be able to enter your orders by computer without calling a broker. If you know what you want to buy or sell, this is the most efficient way to make the transaction.

Having both a traditional and an Internet broker serves a purpose for many investors. Internet brokerages charge lower fees than traditional brokerages, but they provide fewer services. A traditional brokerage may offer participation in an initial public offering (IPO) to longtime customers. A traditional broker will send literature that may not be available from the Internet broker. And a traditional broker will provide face-to-face consultation which may not be available from an Internet broker. The key to using the two types of brokerages effectively is learning how to divide your business and your contacts between the two brokerages.

Message Boards

One of the interesting features of having a brokerage account on the Internet is the message boards that are available to stockholders and to anyone wishing to participate. The basic purpose of the boards is to allow a free exchange of comments on a company's operations and prospects. A secondary purpose is to provide the opportunity for presenting opinions on the future direction of the stock price.

The people who participate can be divided into several classes. The highest-class participant is one who has researched the company thoroughly and shares knowledge with other participants. Based on his or her comments, this person gradually gains the respect of those who read the contributions. Another high-class type of contributor is skilled in technical analysis and shares an opinion on the current action of the stock price and its future direction. However, some people who make comments about stock price patterns are not skilled analysts, and it is best to check out the validity of any such analysis before taking any action. Refer to Chapter 2 to determine the accuracy of analytical comments on stock price patterns.

In summary, message boards comments can be interesting and educational or mundane or, worse, misleading. Read them for whatever value they may have, but make no transactions solely on the basis of a message board comment.

Pitfalls to Avoid

When a stock is trading for less than a dollar a share, it may *seem* like a bargain. Because of their very low prices, they are referred to as "penny stocks." They are enticing, but speculating in this category of stocks is dangerous. While the price is low, the risk factor is extremely high. These stocks are priced in pennies because investors realize there is very little value in them. The worst feeling an investor can have is to watch his or her stock approach or reach zero.

Another temptation for some investors is a stock that is rising at a very fast pace. It gets a lot of favorable publicity as it makes new high after new high. Many investors feel tempted to go along on this joyride, but this is a dangerous high risk because stocks that have risen a long way can fall just as far. The best time to buy a stock is when it is just getting started in an uptrend.

When a stock goes into a downtrend, it gives stockholders the difficult choice of whether to sell or hold on for a recovery. Some investors find it hard to sell a stock that has performed well, and they hold on while their paper profits disappear. No matter how well you have done with a stock, when the price goes down through the 200-day moving average, it's time to sell and look for other opportunities.

Progress Review

At least once a year, review your progress to see if you are on schedule to achieve your financial goal for retirement. If you are not satisfied with the gains you have made, determine the causes of the deficiency by considering the following questions:

- *Are you taking an appropriate level of risk during the bullish phase of the stock market?* Perhaps you have been too conservative in selecting investments during this phase. Companies that are in new, growing industries generally produce higher capital gains than those in established or mature industries. Look for stocks that have a moving average with an angle of ascent that is between 20 and 35 degrees. Finding these stocks in the early phase of a bull market will provide sustainable capital appreciation.

- *Are you waiting too long to switch into a money market fund or zero coupon bonds when the market goes into a bearish phase?* Gains made in a bull market disappear quickly when a bear market begins. To detect the start of a bear market, look for a developing topping pattern as an early warning sign. Then watch for the price to penetrate down through its 200-day moving average. When that occurs, it's time to convert your paper profits into capital gains.

- *Are you selecting companies that are growing slowly or not at all?* Companies go through several phases. The first phase displays fast growth because there are few companies competing for the available revenues. When more companies recognize the profit opportunities in the industry, they enter the competition and profit margins stop increasing. The final phase is when growth has stopped because the industry is crowded with too many companies fighting for the available customers. Profit margins shrink, and some companies in the industry show losses instead of profits. Before purchasing stock in a company, ascertain which phase the industry is in and give preference to companies in growing industries.

- *Have you placed too high a percentage of your assets in one investment?* When you first discover a company that appears to have terrific prospects, you may be tempted to buy more than a reasonable amount of shares. By concentrating too much of your assets in one investment, you increase the risk level. Spreading your assets among different types of investments creates a diversified portfolio that controls the level of risk.

To be successful at investing, follow these guidelines:

- Generate your own investment ideas based on independent thinking.
- Be wary of advisors and other professionals who have interests that are different from yours.
- Conduct your own research before making any purchases.
- Distinguish between television shows that are genuinely informative and those that are primarily entertainment.
- Divide your business appropriately between traditional and Internet brokerages.
- Diversify your investments to lower the level of risk.
- Review your winners and losers and learn from both.

Chapter 9

Portfolio Management for Ages 40 to 45

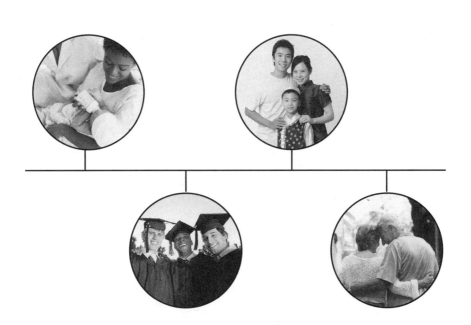

Introduction

The objectives for this period are superior capital gains and high dividends. This combination has proved to be very rewarding to investors over the long run. It is also a good tactic to keep a low-risk component in your portfolio. The Barclays fund that tracks the S&P index of 400 medium-sized companies that represent both growth and value provides this element. The stock ticker symbol for this fund is IJH.

In the previous five-year period, you held up to 10 companies selected for their ability to increase earnings. You now have a track record to review for each company. Identify those that have performed the best and retain them. The poorer performers should be sold and replaced by selecting new growth companies.

Selecting New Winners

A good source for finding companies with high potential for capital gains is *Investor's Business Daily* Monday edition. Obtain a copy at your public library or elsewhere. Refer to the break page that starts the second section of the newspaper which shows the first 20 stock price charts of 100 high-performance companies. Several steps must be followed to find the companies to replace those you sell.

All 100 of these companies have been evaluated by *Investor's Business Daily* as having good fundamental characteristics. Since this screening has already been done, your main objective will be to find those that have positive stock price and moving average relationships. As you make your choices, do not select any that are in the same industries as those companies you are holding. This will keep your portfolio of individual stocks diversified and the risk level lower. Make notes of the industries your current stocks are in. As you select each new company, refer to the list to ensure there is no duplication.

Next, survey each chart of the first 20 companies and look for the stock price that is consistently above its moving average. Check the angle of ascent in the right half of the chart because that time period reflects the most current data. If you have a protractor, use it to measure the angle. It should be between 20 and 35 degrees because these are angles of ascent that are sustainable in the long term.

Then check the bars at the bottom of the chart that indicate the volume of trading. In the ideal pattern, the trading volume increases as the stock price rises. After you find several charts that meet both of these standards, make a list of the stock symbols. This next step in the process is required to assure the exclusivity of industry for each company.

Go to the Internet Web site Finance.Yahoo.com. Enter each symbol one at a time in the search slot. From the menu select "Competitors." Note the symbol and name of each competitive company. If any of those are already in your portfolio, eliminate the candidate company. Continue this process until you have replaced all the companies you sold and do not have two companies in the same industry. If you do not have enough new companies to replace those you sold, return to the list of 100 companies in *Investor's Business Daily* and continue your search through the companies numbered 21 through 100.

If you don't have access to a copy of *Investor's Business Daily*, an alternative source to explore is *Barron's* weekly magazine. The pull-out section is titled, "Market Week." Look for the New York Stock Exchange Composite List. This gives the name of the company; stock ticker symbol; yield; price-to- earnings ratio; last price of the preceding week; amount of change in the price; the earnings for the latest year, this year, and next year; and the amount of the dividend. Unlike *Investor's Business Daily*, these companies have not been prequalified on a fundamental basis. Therefore this investigation will need both a fundamental and technical aspect. Here is the procedure for checking the basic fundamental data.

First, select several companies you are interested in from the list. Check the yield and look for 6 percent or higher and make sure the earnings projected for next year are higher than this year's earnings. Make a list of the companies' symbols. Go to Finance.Yahoo.com Web site and enter each symbol into the search slot. Click on "Key Statistics" in the menu at the left. Then check for these qualifying features:

- The forward price-to-earnings ratio should be 17 to 1 or lower.
- The operating profit margin should be 10 percent or higher.
- Total cash should be higher than debt.

Make a list of the stock symbols for the companies that qualify. The next step is to do a technical analysis of their stock price charts. Go to StockCharts.com. Click on the drop down menu icon and select "Gallery View." Enter each symbol in the search slot and click "Go." A daily chart appears first. Scroll down to see a weekly chart. The charts show a 200-day moving average or a 40-week moving average, which are the same time period. The stock price should be above the average, and the larger the gap, the better. The moving average should be rising at an angle of at least 10 degrees. If you have a protractor, use it to measure the angle. Another positive relationship is if the price has just penetrated up through the moving average. This indicates a change of momentum to the upside and is very favorable. The final item to check is the volume of trading, which is at the bottom of the chart. The ideal condition is if the trading volume is increasing as the stock price is rising. After finding several companies that qualify both on fundamental and technical factors, check each company to make sure it is in an industry different from the other companies.

To do this, go to Finance.Yahoo.com and click on "Competitors" after entering the symbol for each new company in the search slot. When the display of competitors appears, check to make sure that none of the other companies appears in that listing.

ClearStation Web Site

Here is another way the Internet can be helpful in finding investment-worthy companies. Go to ClearStation.com. On the right side of the home page is the title "Hot Industries." This list shows the three or four industries that have been outperforming all others. This listing is revised frequently. Check it periodically until you see an industry different from the ones you have in your stock portfolio. Click on that industry and a list of companies' symbols appears. They are ranked by relative strength. (See column labeled "RS Rating.") This refers to their price performance during the preceding 13 weeks versus the average performance of all companies in the industry. Start at the top of the list and make a note of several of the symbols. Then go to the Finance.Yahoo.com Web site and repeat the procedure described above to evaluate the fundamental condition of the company.

As you follow the procedure, the key items to search for are

- The forward price-to-earnings ratio is 20 or lower.
- The operating profit margin is 10 percent or higher.
- Total cash is higher than the debt.
- The dividend yield is at least 6 percent.

This last item ensures that your portfolio of stocks will achieve the objective of producing high income flow during this phase of the plan.

Bull Market Portfolio

After you have assembled your revised portfolio of companies, you will have your investments for a bull market phase. It will consist of 10 companies that have sound fundamentals and whose stocks have technical patterns that project price advances in the future. This part of the portfolio will accomplish the objectives of superior capital gains with high income. The other half of the portfolio is the Barclays fund, symbol IJH. It tracks the S&P index of 400 medium-sized companies that have been selected because they have grown or because they are currently undervalued. Because the fund contains these two types of companies, it is called a *blended fund*.

Range-Bound Market Portfolio

If a range-bound market comes after a bull market, you might decide to continue to hold the individual stocks you previously selected. However, if during the bull market some stocks performed poorly, you should sell them and repeat the selection process. You will then have a diversified portfolio of growth companies to hold during the range-bound market.

The Barclays fund that tracks the performance of the S&P index of 400 stocks would not gain much during a range-bound market because the market averages generally remain flat during that market condition. Sell the Barclays fund (IJH) and replace it with a real estate investment trust fund (REIT). A list of such funds can be found in Chapter 6 in the section titled "REIT Fund Properties." This list gives the names and properties in the funds along with their dividend yield rates. By switching to a REIT fund, you will have a high income flow and an opportunity for a capital gain if property values increase during the range-bound market.

Bear Market Portfolio

If a bear market develops after the range-bound or bull markets, sell all individual stocks and your fund. Put the money into the brokerage's money market fund. If you can get a higher yield from one-year U.S. zero coupon bonds, buy those to wait for the end of the bear market. If the bear market ends before the bonds mature, you can sell them at any time. If the bear market continues beyond the maturity date of the bond, use the proceeds to buy bonds that mature in three months' time.

Suggested Portfolio Contents

Shown below is a summary of the portfolio contents you would have during bull, bear, and range-bound markets during this time phase. Use this display as a reference to guide your portfolio adjustments when the market switches from one phase to another.

Bull Market	
Objectives	Superior capital gains and high-dividend income
Risk Levels	Moderate for individual stocks; low for Barclays fund
Suggestions	Ten medium-sized companies with high dividends, 50 percent
	Barclays fund (IJH), 50 percent
Range-Bound Market	
Objectives	High dividends with some capital gains
Risk Levels	Moderate for individual stocks; low for REIT fund
Suggestions	Ten medium-sized growth companies, 50 percent
	REIT fund, 50 percent
Bear Market	
Objectives	Preserve capital and receive income
Risk Levels	None for zero coupon bonds; very low for money market fund
Suggestions	Brokerage's money market fund, 100 percent
	or
	U.S. zero coupon bonds, 100 percent

Chapter 10

Portfolio Management for Ages 45 to 50

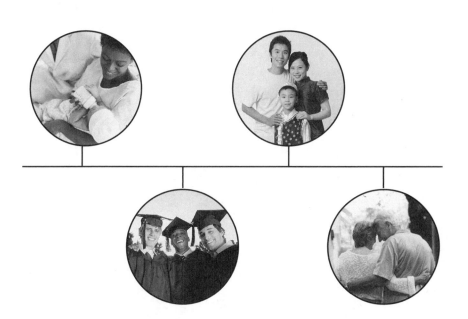

Introduction

This is a transitional phase. In the earlier years, your primary objective was large capital gains which required moderate tolerance for risk. Your secondary objective was high income flow, and this goal remains unchanged. In the years that follow these five years, your primary objective will be to seek a level of capital gains consistent with a low level of risk. During these five years, you should gradually reduce your holdings of individual companies and switch into investments with lower risk levels. This chapter provides guidelines for doing this.

Assessing Risk Level

The best way to sell your stocks is one at a time after an assessment of each one's level of risk and potential reward. However, if a bear market starts, you should sell them quickly. Since assessing risk is a subjective activity, it's important to have an objective source to help in the process. Fortunately the Internet provides a convenient aid at Web site Moneycentral.msn.com. At the home page click on "Investing." On the tool bar click on "Stocks." Under the "Research Tools," click on "StockScouter." Enter the symbol of one stock and click "Go."

You now have access to the objective opinion of the analysts whose work is shown on this site. Read the Quick Summary and then note the Expected Risk/Return illustration on the right side of the screen. Compare each of your stocks to all the others. The most important item to note in this display is whether the risk bar or the reward bar is longer. Stocks whose risk bars are much longer than their reward bars are the ones you should sell first. Within that group of higher-risk stocks, identify the one with the longest risk bar and make it your prime candidate to sell. The next decision is when to sell it. You can decide this on the basis of the guidelines in Chapter 2. For example, if the price is in a downtrend or it has just gone down through the 200-day moving average, it should be sold immediately. This procedure for evaluating the risk level of all the stocks should be done periodically and a ranking should be set up and revised periodically. After each sale you will have money for lower-risk investments. Options for more conservative investing are described in the following section.

Municipal Bonds

Municipal bonds are sold by states, municipalities, toll roads, housing authorities, etc., to finance revenue-producing projects. Buyers of those bonds are promised interest payments until the bonds are called or reach maturity. The income from the toll roads, etc., is used to make the interest payments and to return the amount invested to the bondholders. Some bonds are issued by a state and payments are guaranteed by the state. These are called "General Obligation" bonds. They are the safest type of municipal bonds. In general, municipal bonds, whether issued by a state, municipality, toll road, or other type of authority, are a relatively low-risk investment.

An investor can buy a single municipal bond or purchase a municipal bond fund, which owns many different bonds. There are two main types of municipal bond funds. Single-state bond funds confine their purchases to the bonds issued by one state. National bond funds purchase bonds from many states in order to diversify and benefit from high interest rates where they are available. Whether single state or national, these funds are closed-end which means they can be bought and sold when the stock market is open. The primary reason to buy bonds is for the income they provide. They are referred to as fixed-income investments because they produce a reliable stream of income for the duration of the bond. Individual municipal bonds make interest payments twice a year. Closed-end municipal bond funds pay monthly, and many investors prefer these more frequent payments. *Barron's* weekly magazine has a closed-end fund section that lists all of the municipal bond funds. For each fund the following information is shown:

- The exchange on which it is traded
- The net asset value (NAV)
- The most recent market price
- How much of a premium or discount there is between the market price and the net asset value
- The amount of yield delivered during the preceding 12 months

NOTE

There is usually a discrepancy between the net asset value of a fund and its market price. When the market price is lower than the net asset value, you are able to buy the fund at discount. When the market price is above the net asset value, you pay a premium price if you buy it. The following section presents detailed information on national municipal bond fund portfolios.

National Municipal Bond Funds

The following national municipal bond funds were taken from the list in *Barron's* section on closed-end funds. They were selected because they pay high dividends. Also, prior to this book's publication date, they were available at a discount from their net asset value. For current Morningstar ratings, go to Morningstar.com. Morningstar is a fund rating company. The highest rating is five stars; the lowest rating is one star.

DWS Strategic Municipal Income Trust trades on the New York Stock Exchange under ticker symbol KSM. The primary objective of this fund is to obtain a high level of income for the fund holders. At this book's publication time, the dividend yield was approximately 6 percent. The secondary objective of the fund is to have income exempt from regular federal income taxes. The fund's top holdings are bonds issued by authorities in Texas (15 percent), New York (10 percent), California (6 percent), Illinois (6 percent), and Massachusetts (5 percent). Fifteen percent of the bonds are general obligations. The other 85 percent produce revenue from toll roads, hospitals, leases, and state or municipality operations. The fund is under the control of the asset management division of DWS Scudder Deutsche Bank Group. Mr. Phillip Condon is the portfolio manager of the fund. He has 26 years of professional investment management experience.

BlackRock MuniHoldings Fund II, Incorporated, is listed on the New York Stock Exchange, and it trades under the ticker symbol MUH. The primary objective of the fund is to provide high income that is exempt from regular federal income taxes. At publication time, the dividend was approximately 6 percent. Its main holdings are bonds issued by California (15 percent), Virginia (9 percent), New York (8 percent), New Jersey (7 percent), and Texas (7 percent). General obligation bonds comprise 37 percent of its holdings. It usually trades at a discount from the market price, but at times its price moves to a premium. This gives the fund holder the opportunity for a capital gain. The fund is managed by a team of fixed-income analysts under the jurisdiction of Merrill Lynch Investments.

DWS Municipal Income Trust trades on the New York Stock Exchange under the symbol KTF. The objective of the fund is to provide income exempt from federal income tax. At publication time, the dividend was 6 percent. Twenty-six percent of its holdings are general obligation bonds issued by states. The top five holdings are issued by Texas (12 percent), California (10 percent), New York (8 percent), New Jersey (8 percent), and Illinois (6 percent). The fund is geographically diversified by virtue of having more than 150 bonds issued from different parts of the United States. The ratings of 90 percent of its bonds are AAA (73 percent), AA (7 percent), and A (10 percent). The fund is managed by Mr. Phillip Condon who has 26 years of professional investment experience. The fund is under the control of the Scudder Deutsche Bank Group.

Eaton Vance Municipal Income Trust is traded on the New York Stock Exchange under the symbol EVN. The objective of the fund is to produce high income for its fund holders, but 24 percent of its assets are subject to the alternative minimum tax.

At publication time, the dividend was approximately 6 percent. The top holdings are bonds issued by North Carolina Municipal Power Agency (6.5 percent), NYC IDA Special Facility Authority American Airlines/JFK (8 percent), Brazos River Authority, Texas-CenterPoint Energy (7.75 percent), and Henderson, Nevada Catholic Healthcare West (5.6 percent). It holds more than 100 bond issues spread geographically across the United States. The portfolio has been managed by Thomas Metzold, CFA, for more than 15 years. Eaton Vance Investments has been managing municipal bond funds for more than 50 years.

BlackRock MuniHoldings Fund, Incorporated, trades on the New York Stock Exchange under the symbol MHD. The objective of the fund is to provide fund holders with high income exempt from regular federal income tax. At the time of publication, the dividend yield was approximately 6 percent. The fund usually trades at a discount from its net asset value. Occasionally the price goes above net asset value, which presents an opportunity for a capital gain. General obligation bonds represent 32 percent of the portfolio. The top five holdings of the fund are bonds issued by California (12 percent), Texas (10 percent), New York (9 percent), New Jersey (8 percent), and Florida (7 percent). The fund is managed by a team at BlackRock Investments.

Nuveen Dividend Advantage Municipal Fund trades on the New York Stock Exchange under the symbol NAD. The objective of the fund is to provide fund holders with high income exempt from regular federal income taxes. As of the date of publication, the fund is paying a dividend of approximately 6 percent. Top holdings are bonds issued by Regional Transportation Authority of Illinois, Illinois Development Financial Authority, Philadelphia Airport Facilities, Florida State Board of Education and Michigan Hospital Financing Authority. The fund is managed by Nuveen Investments.

BlackRock MuniVest Fund Incorporated trades on the American Stock Exchange under the symbol MVF. The objective of this fund is to provide high income that is exempt from the regular federal income tax. The fund pays a dividend of approximately 6 percent. Thirty-one percent of its bond holdings are general obligations of the states that issued them. The top five investments in its portfolio are bonds issued by Texas (11 percent), Illinois (10 percent), New York (10 percent), California (10 percent), and Indiana (6 percent). The fund is managed by a team at BlackRock Investments.

Bull Market Portfolio

During this five-year transitional period, you will be selling your individual stocks gradually and buying shares in national municipal bond funds as the proceeds become available. Also sell the Barclays fund that tracks the performance of the S&P 400 index of medium-sized growth and value stocks, symbol IJH. Replace it with the Barclays fund that tracks the performance of the S&P index of 400 medium-sized stocks selected for value. The symbol is IJJ.

RANGE-BOUND MARKET PORTFOLIO

A range-bound market is one where the S&P index of 500 stocks fluctuates above and below and in close proximity to its 200-day moving average. If this condition develops, your primary objectives become high income flow with some capital gain. This goal is best achieved by switching from the Barclays fund to a real estate investment trust (REIT) fund. A list of these funds was provided in Chapter 6. When you are ready to make the purchase, select a fund from that list or find another REIT fund at Investinreits.com. You would then be holding a mix of dividend-paying growth stocks, a national municipal bond fund, and a REIT fund for the duration of the range-bound market.

Bear Market Portfolio

If a bear market follows a bull or range-bound market, sell any remaining individual stocks and the REIT fund. Put the money into your brokerage's money market fund or buy one-year zero coupon bonds. If you are getting high dividends from the national municipal bond fund, hold it for the monthly income.

Suggested Portfolio Contents

Here is a summary of the three portfolios that show the changes necessary to adapt to the bull, range-bound, and bear market conditions. Use this display as a reference to guide your transactions during this five-year period.

Bull Market

Objectives	High income flow with low risk
Risk Levels	Moderate for individual stocks; low for Barclays fund
Suggestions	Assess risk levels and sell high-risk stocks
	Sell Barclays fund, IJH
	Buy Barclays fund, IJJ
	Buy national municipal bond fund

Range-Bound Market

Objective	High income with some capital gains
Risk Factor	Moderate for individual stocks; low for REIT fund; low for municipal bond fund
Suggestions	Medium-sized companies paying high dividends
	National municipal bond fund
	REIT fund

Bear Market

Objective	Preserve capital and receive income
Risk Levels	Very low for brokerage's money market fund; low for municipal bond fund; none for U.S. zero coupon bonds
Suggestions	Brokerage's money market
	or
	One-year maturity zero coupon bonds
	National municipal bond fund

Chapter 11

Portfolio Management
for Ages 50 to 55

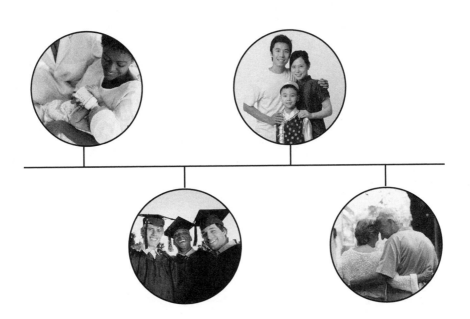

Introduction

Utility companies are an appropriate investment at this stage because they provide high dividends and the potential for capital gains at a low level of risk. They supply the power which supports our modern lifestyle and all forms of industrial production. The demand for these services has been growing steadily since the start of the Industrial Revolution. Although there are some projects under way to develop alternative sources of power, they will not present significant competition to the traditional utilities for a long time. Utilities are a regulated industry because each one has an effective monopoly over its geographic area of operation. These considerations make utility companies one of the most conservative type of investments.

Some utility companies pay dividends that are less than half of their net income. If their income declines slightly at times because of unseasonable weather or other reasons, they can maintain dividend payments because of the large amounts of cash on their balance sheets. Investors looking for a recession-resistant source of income hold shares in a utility company to meet their need for reliable cash flow.

Utility Companies

The utility companies in the following list have been selected based on certain criteria. Their earnings are between 20 percent and 75 percent higher than their dividends, and this surplus provides the capacity for the payout to be raised. Their operating profit margins are between 10 percent and 21 percent. This indicates that the companies are maintaining effective control over expenses. Their price-to-earnings ratios are 15 to 1 or lower, which implies their stocks are selling at reasonable prices relative to their capability to produce earnings. And their 200-day moving averages were all in uptrends of 10 degrees or higher at the time of publication.

To check on current stock prices and moving average trends, go to StockCharts.com. Click on the drop down menu icon and select "Gallery View." Enter a stock symbol in the search slot and click "Go." Check the slope of the 200-day moving average in the daily chart to see if it is slanting upward by at least 10 degrees. Also check to make sure the price has remained above the moving average consistently. These technical features identify stocks that have long-term upward price momentum based on increasing revenue and earnings.

Great Plains Energy Incorporated trades on the New York Stock Exchange under the ticker symbol GXP. It distributes and wholesales electricity to other utilities and major industrial users. It also retails electricity to commercial, institutional, and manufacturing companies and residences in California, Maryland, New York, Ohio, New Jersey, Pennsylvania, Texas, Missouri, and Kansas.

Great Plains Energy pays a dividend of 5 percent. It has an earnings surplus that is 25 percent higher than the dividend payment. Its operating profit margin is 10 percent. It has a record of increasing net income over the long term. It has a price-to-earnings ratio of 15 to 1, which puts its stock price at a reasonable level. For more information, visit its home page at Greatplainsenergy.com.

Consolidated Edison trades on the New York Stock Exchange under the symbol ED. It provides electricity in New York City and Westchester County and gas service in Manhattan, the Bronx, Queens, and Westchester. It also provides electricity in southeastern New York state and adjacent areas of New Jersey and Pennsylvania. In addition it sells electricity to other utilities in the northeast and mid-Atlantic regions of the United States.

Consolidated Edison pays a dividend of 5 percent. It has an earnings surplus of 28 percent over this payment. It has an operating profit margin of 13 percent. It has a record of increasing net income over the long term. It has a price-to-earnings ratio of 15 to 1, which implies the stock is selling at a reasonable level. For more information on this company, visit its home page at Conedison.com.

TECO Energy trades on the New York Stock Exchange under the symbol TE. It is a diversified energy company with operations in electricity, natural gas, coal processing, and synthetic fuel. The company provides electricity and natural gas to 645,000 and 321,000 customers, respectively, in Florida. It engages in coal processing and synthetic fuel production in Kentucky, Tennessee, and Virginia. It also participates in power projects and electric distribution in Guatemala.

TECO Energy pays a dividend of 5 percent. Its dividend is covered by an earnings surplus of 28 percent. It has an operating profit margin of 13 percent and a record of increasing earnings over the long term. Its price-to-earnings ratio is 16 to 1, which implies the stock is selling at a reasonable level. For further information on the company, visit its home page at Tecoenergy.com.

Westar Energy Inc., trades on the New York Stock Exchange under the symbol WR. It wholesales electricity to 48 cities and 4 electric cooperatives in Kansas. It also supplies electricity to residential, commercial, and industrial retail customers in northeastern Kansas. It has approximately 660,000 retail customers.

Westar Energy pays a dividend of 4.5 percent. Its earnings are 75 percent higher than its dividend payments. This large surplus allows for an increase in the size of the dividend. It has an operating profit margin of 18 percent and a record of increasing earnings over the long term. It has a price-to-earnings ratio of 13 to 1, which implies a reasonable stock price level. For more information on the company visit Westarenergy.com.

Xcel Energy, Inc., trades on the New York Stock Exchange under the symbol XEL. It operates as an electricity and natural gas company and sells to residential, commercial, industrial, public authorities, and wholesale customers. It provides electricity to approximately 3,250,000 customers and natural gas to approximately 1,750,000 users in Colorado, Kansas, Michigan, Minnesota, New Mexico, North Dakota, South Dakota, Oklahoma, Texas, and Wisconsin.

Xcel Energy pays a dividend of 4.5 percent and has earnings 50 percent higher than the payments. It has an operating profit margin of 11 percent. Its price-to-earnings ratio is 15 to 1, which puts the stock at a reasonable price level. For more information, visit the home page at Xcelenergy.com.

CenterPoint Energy, Inc., trades on the New York Stock Exchange under the symbol CNP. It provides electricity wholesale to municipalities, electric cooperatives, distribution companies, and retail electric providers. It also provides natural gas to residential, commercial, and industrial customers in Arkansas, Louisiana, Minnesota, Mississippi, Oklahoma, and Texas. It sells natural gas supplies to commercial and industrial customers and to electric and gas utilities. And it provides transportation services to shippers and end users.

CenterPoint Energy pays a dividend of 5 percent. Its earnings are more than double that level, which provides the flexibility to raise the dividend. Its operating profit margin is 10 percent. Its net income has increased significantly over the long term. Its price-to-earnings ratio is 11 to 1, which puts the stock price at a relatively low level. For more information on CenterPoint Energy, visit its home page at Centerpointenergy.com.

Southern Company trades on the New York Stock Exchange under the symbol SO. It sells electricity retail to customers in Alabama, Georgia, Florida, and Mississippi. It also has investments in synthetic fuels, telecommunications, and natural gas. It has approximately 4,000,000 customers.

Southern Company pays a dividend of 4.5 percent. Its earnings exceed the rate of dividend payments by 30 percent. Its operating profit margin is 21 percent. Its net income has increased over the long term. Its price-to-earnings ratio is 15 to 1, which makes the stock a reasonable investment. For more information on the company, visit its home page at Southernco.com.

DTE Energy Company trades on the New York Stock Exchange under the symbol DTE. Its Electric Utility division sells electricity to 2,200,000 residential, commercial, industrial, and wholesale customers in Michigan. Its Gas Utility division sells natural gas to 1,300,000 residential, commercial, and industrial customers in that state. It also gathers and transmits natural gas through pipelines in the lower peninsula of Michigan. Its Non-Utility Operations division manages synfuel projects and waste coal recovery operations, coal transportation, and storage.

DTE Energy Company pays a dividend of 5 percent. It has earnings that are 30 percent higher than the dividend rate. Its operating profit margin is 10 percent. It has a record of increasing its net income over the long term. It has a price-to-earnings ratio of 14 to 1, which puts the stock at a reasonable price level. For more information on this company, visit Dteenergy.com.

Integrys Energy Group trades on the New York Stock Exchange under the symbol TEG. It provides electric power to municipal utilities, electric cooperatives, energy marketers, and municipal joint action agencies in Michigan's Upper Peninsula. It also sells natural gas to 300 municipalities in northeastern Wisconsin and Michigan. It provides energy management and consultant services to retail and wholesale customers in the northeastern quadrant of the United States and adjacent portions of Canada.

Integrys pays a dividend of 4.6 percent. Its earnings are 75 percent above the dividend rate. Its operating profit margin is 10 percent. It has a record of increasing its net income over the long term. Its price-to-earnings ratio is 12 to 1, which makes the stock price very reasonable. For more information on the company, visit Integrysgroup.com.

Utility Funds

Utility funds invest in groups of utility companies. A utility fund is a more conservative investment than a single company. Utility funds generally hold 15 or more utility companies which are diversified among the types of fuel used by utilities: oil, natural gas, coal, nuclear, synfuel, and water power. Some of the utility plants can switch between oil and natural gas and use the one that is less expensive. Here is information on some utility funds.

1. Eaton Vance Utilities fund, Class A, trades on the Nasdaq under the symbol EVTMX. It has a price-to-earnings ratio of 15 to 1 and pays a dividend of approximately 2.5 percent. The Morningstar fund rating is the maximum five stars. The minimum purchase amount is $1,000.

2. Jennison Utility and Telecom trades on the Nasdaq under the symbol PRUZX. It has a price-to-earnings ratio of 17 to 1 and pays a dividend of approximately 2.5 percent. The minimum purchase amount is $10,000. Morningstar gives this fund a rating of five stars.

3. Franklin Utilities, Class A, trades on the Nasdaq with the symbol FKUTX. It has a price-to-earnings ratio of 17 to 1 and pays a dividend of approximately 3.0 percent. The minimum purchase amount is $100,000. This fund has a Morningstar rating of three stars.

Bull Market Portfolio

From this time forward it is important to ensure the investments you make are very conservative. Your main objectives now are to preserve your assets and get reliable income with low risk. In line with these objectives, sell any remaining medium-sized companies you still own. Switch into one or more of the utility companies or funds listed above. Also, sell the Barclays fund that tracks the S&P index of 400 medium-sized companies. To replace it, purchase the Barclays fund that tracks the S&P index of 500 large growth companies, symbol IVW. These companies are well established within their industries and have proven track records.

Range-Bound Market Portfolio

If the market becomes range-bound, switch out of the Barclays fund and purchase a real estate investment trust fund. You may want to continue holding the utility stocks and fund for the monthly income they provide.

Bear Market Portfolio

If a bear market starts, you should sell the REIT fund but continue holding the utility stocks and fund for the income. Put the money from the sale of the REIT fund into the brokerage's money market fund or into U.S. zero coupon bonds. Ask the broker which one provides the better return and make your decision on that basis.

Suggested Portfolio Contents

Here's how your new, more conservative posture is reflected in the three different portfolios you may need in these five years.

Bull Market

Objectives	Preserve capital, receive high dividend income, and make some capital gains
Risk Levels	Low for Barclays large company fund; very low for utility stocks and fund
Selections	Barclays fund of large growth companies, symbol IVW, 50 percent
	Utility stocks and fund, 50 percent

Range-Bound Market

Objectives	High, reliable income with low risk and some capital gain
Risk Levels	Low for REIT fund; very low for utility stocks and fund
Suggestions	REIT fund, 50 percent
	Utility stocks and fund, 50 percent

Bear Market

Objectives	Preserve capital and receive income flow
Risk Levels	None for U.S. bonds; very low for money market fund; low for utility stocks and fund
Suggestions	Short-term zero coupon bonds, 50 percent
	or
	Brokerage's money market fund, 50 percent
	Utility stocks and fund, 50 percent

Chapter 12

Portfolio Management for Ages 55 to 60

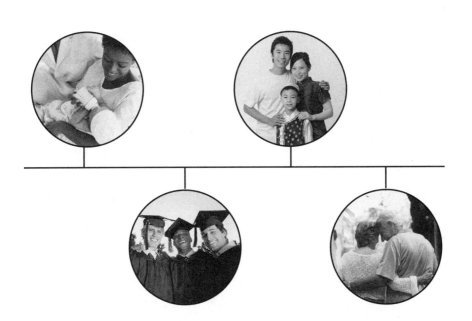

Introduction

As you get closer to retirement age, it's important to be very conservative and risk averse. During these years you also need to ensure the continuity of high income. These objectives can be achieved by adding preferred stocks to your portfolio.

Characteristics of Preferred Issues

Preferred stocks are issued and sold by corporations to raise cash for expanding the company's operations and for other purposes. Some corporations have more than one issue of preferred stock. In these cases each preferred issue is given a letter to distinguish it, e.g., A, B, C, etc.

The dividend rate on a preferred issue is usually higher than that received by holders of common stock. The company must pay dividends to the preferred stockholders before any dividends can be paid on the common stock. The company that sells a preferred issue promises to pay the dividends and refund the issue price if the stock is called. For this reason, a preferred stock is more like a bond than a common stock.

When a common stock is issued, there is no requirement that it pay a dividend and there is no commitment to any price level. The price can fluctuate widely in response to changes in the relationship between the supply of shares offered for sale and the demand for shares of the stock from buyers.

The market price of preferred stocks usually stays close to the issue price which is most often set at $25 per share. Although preferred stocks are bought for their high dividends, they can also be traded for capital gains. This possibility occurs when shares are purchased at a discount and later the market price reaches a premium over par value. For example, a preferred stock issued at a par value of $25 per share may trade below that price if adverse market conditions develop after the issue date. If conditions later become favorable to the company, the price may go above $25. The investor who buys a preferred issue at a discount can make a capital gain by selling the stock if it trades above par value or when it is called at par.

Investing in Preferred Issues

Preferred issues are traded on the New York, American, and Nasdaq stock exchanges. In order to get a quote on a preferred stock, it is necessary to know the prescribed format since it varies among Web sites. On the Finance.Yahoo site, the format is XYZ-PA. Note the dash after the ticker symbol of the company. The *P* stands for preferred and the final letter designates the specific preferred issue. On the QuantumOnline Web site, the format is XYZ-A. The *P* for preferred is not used. The TDAmeritrade Internet brokerage uses the same format as QuantumOnline. Other online brokerages may use a different format. To get a quote or make a transaction, you will need to learn what it is.

Preferred issues are relatively resistant to the negative effects of an economic recession compared to the common stock of the issuing company. The companies in the list below were selected on the basis of the following factors:

- They pay dividends of at least 6 percent.
- Standard & Poor's rating service gives them the investment grade ratings of AAA, AA, A, or BBB.
- The call date does not imply an obligation to call the issue.
- They are listed on the New York Stock Exchange.

NOTE

To get current financial data on a company that issues preferred stocks, go to Finance.Yahoo.com, enter the symbol and click on menu items "Summary," "Key Statistics," and "Income Statement," and evaluate the data provided. To assess the competitive position of the issuing company, click on "Competitors." To get information on the preferred issue itself, go to QuantumOnline.com, enter the symbol with the letter designator in the slot, and click "Search." Review the description of the preferred issue. Then click on "Click for current price quote from the NYSE."

Equity Residential Properties (EQR) is a REIT. It is the largest publicly traded company specializing in rental apartment communities. It owns or has investments in more than 90 properties in 34 states. It has more than 200,000 rental units that cover a wide range of tastes and income levels. All of their communities are in convenient locations. They have clubhouses, pools, tennis courts, and other recreational facilities. They offer a "Rent With Equity" program that allows lessees to earn credit toward the purchase of their condominium. *Fortune* magazine named them one of America's most admired companies.

Equity Residential Properties' preferred stock issue D pays dividends on 1/15, 4/15, 7/15, and 10/15. The rate of the dividend is approximately 8 percent. The annual dividend amount is $2.15 per year for each share of preferred stock.

HRPT Properties (HRP) is a REIT which owns and leases more than 280 office buildings and 135 industrial properties in 31 states. They lease many of their properties to the U.S. government and to the medical profession. They also own and lease a large industrial complex in Oahu, Hawaii. Their leases, some of which run 10 years, produce a steady flow of earnings.

HRPT's preferred stock issue B pays dividends on 2/15, 5/15, 8/15, and 11/15. The dividend rate is approximately 8 percent. The annual dividend is $2.1875 for each share of preferred stock.

Public Storage Inc. (PSA) is a REIT that acquires, develops, owns, and operates storage facilities. It also has ancillary operations of leasing storage containers, renting trucks, and selling boxes and other packaging supplies. The company has 1,400 properties in 37 states with 839,000 rentable units. It has an operating profit margin of 40 percent because expenses associated with the storage business are very low.

Public Storage's preferred stock issue T pays dividends on 3/31, 6/30, 9/30, and 12/31. The dividend rate is approximately 7.5 percent which amounts to $1.90 per share of preferred stock annually.

Vornado Realty Trust (VNO) is a diversified REIT. It owns and leases office properties, retail outlets, showroom space, cold storage facilities, warehouses, toy stores, and hotel properties. It has 111 office properties in the high rent districts of the New York metropolitan area and Washington, D.C. It has ownership interests in industrial installations, and student and military housing. It also makes loans to other real estate–related companies. With this diversified base of revenues, its earnings are very consistent.

Vornado Realty's preferred stock issue series G pays dividends on 1/1, 4/1, 7/1, and 10/1. It pays a dividend of approximately 6.5 percent. The payment amounts to $1.65 per share of preferred stock annually.

First Industrial Realty Trust Inc. (FR) is a REIT which owns, manages, and has under development 100 million square feet of industrial real estate in markets throughout the United States. Its real estate portfolio includes light industrial properties, research and development properties, bulk and regional warehouses, and manufacturing facilities.

First Industrial Realty preferred stock issue J pays dividends on 3/31, 6/30, 9/30, and 12/31. It pays a dividend of approximately 7 percent. The annual payout per preferred share is $1.81.

ProLogis (PLD) is a REIT and is a leading provider of distribution services with 1,727 facilities operating or under development in North America, Japan, and Europe. ProLogis is expanding its global network to increase shareholder value. The company supports customers' expansion plans by adding distribution facilities and services to meet growing demand. ProLogis manages or has under development 204 million square feet of distribution facilities in 99 markets worldwide.

ProLogis preferred stock issue F pays a dividend of approximately 6.5 percent. It distributes the dividends on 3/31, 6/30, 9/30, and 12/31. The annual payout amounts to $1.68 per preferred share.

Duke Realty Corp. (DRE) is a REIT. It develops, manages, and leases offices and industrial parks. Duke's properties total approximately 103 million square feet which accommodates 3,500 tenants. Duke Realty also owns approximately 4,500 acres of undeveloped land that can support 64 million square feet of development. It has 13 operation centers in the Midwest and Southeast United States. It is also currently developing medical offices and retail complexes through its National Development and Construction Group.

Duke Realty's preferred stock issue K pays a dividend of approximately 6.5 percent. It distributes the dividends on 2/28, 5/31, 8/31, and 11/30. The amount of the dividend on each share of preferred is $1.625 per year.

ABN Amro Holding N.V. (ABN) is one of the world's largest banks with more than $520 billion in assets. It has 3,500 offices in over 70 countries. It provides wholesale banking services to financial institutions and public sector clients; retail services to small and medium-sized commercial and consumer clients; and private banking and fund management services to selected organizations and individuals worldwide.

ABN Amro's preferred stock issue E pays a dividend of approximately 6 percent. Payments are made on 3/31, 6/30, 9/30, and 12/31. The amount of the annual payment for each share of preferred stock is $1.475.

JPMorgan Chase & Co. (JPM) is a leading financial services firm with assets of $1.2 trillion. It has offices in 50 countries. It provides investment banking services for consumers and businesses. Its corporate headquarters are in New York City. The firm serves millions of customers in the United States and has many of the world's most prominent institutional and government clients. Its common stock is a component of the Dow Jones Industrial Average.

JPMorgan's preferred stock issue P pays a dividend of about 6.5 percent. It distributes the dividends on 3/1, 6/1, 9/1, and 12/1. It pays $1.5875 for each share of preferred stock annually.

Mid-America Apartment Communities Inc. (MAA) is a REIT that owns apartment communities throughout southeast and south central United States. There are 33,480 rental units in these communities. Each community has a convenient location with extensive facilities and amenities to support an active lifestyle. Professional property managers have authority to adjust the rental charges to meet local market conditions. Because of this flexible approach to leasing the apartments, the communities have an average occupancy rate of approximately 92 percent.

Mid-America Apartment Communities' preferred stock issue H pays a dividend of approximately 8 percent. The dividends are distributed on 3/23, 6/23, 9/23, and 12/23. The annual amount of the payment is $2.075 for each share of preferred stock.

Innkeepers USA Trust (KPA) is a REIT that owns upscale, extended stay hotel properties throughout the United States. It has 67 hotels with approximately 8,100 suites or rooms in 23 states. It has purchased Residence Inn properties and other extended stay hotels to increase their dominance of local markets.

Innkeepers USA's preferred stock issue C pays a dividend of approximately 7.5 percent. It distributes the dividends on the last Tuesday in January, April, July, and October. The annual payout amount is $2 per preferred share.

Bull Market Portfolio

An appropriate bull market portfolio for these five years consists of utility stocks and funds, preferred issues, and the Barclays fund that tracks the performance of the S&P index of 500 stocks blending growth and value. The value stock component of this fund serves to lower the level of risk compared with a fund composed exclusively of growth stocks. Sell the Barclays fund, IVW, and buy its IVV fund. Then review your utility stocks and sell the weakest performers. With that cash buy a few preferred issues from the list above or by researching the QuantumOnline Web site. Your portfolio for a bull market would then consist of Barclays IVV fund, the best-performing utility stocks and selected preferred issues.

Range-Bound Portfolio

If a range-bound market occurs during this period, it's appropriate to switch out of the Barclays fund and into a REIT fund. The Barclays fund would not produce any appreciable capital gains nor a high dividend. The REIT fund will provide high dividends and would have the potential of a capital gain because of its real estate content. Retain the utility stocks, utility fund, and preferred issues.

Bear Market Portfolio

If a bear market develops after a range-bound market, you will need to sell the REIT fund. If a bear market follows a bull market, you will need to sell the Barclays fund. With the proceeds from either sale, you can buy U.S. zero coupon bonds or put the money into the brokerage's money market fund, whichever pays the higher return.

Because preferred issues carry the promise to return par value, you may continue to hold them through bear markets. In the event of a severe recession, the issuing company may have to postpone paying dividends but is obligated to pay them as soon as possible. The term *cumulative* in the description of a preferred issue refers to this commitment. The Web site QuantumOnline.com provides the information on whether the dividends are cumulative for each preferred issue.

Decide if you want to continue holding any utility stocks based on their past performance and their reaction to the bear market. If any go into downtrends, they can be sold and the proceeds switched into preferred issues purchased at a discount.

Suggested Preretirement Portfolio Contents

Preferred stock issues represent an asset class that exhibits price stability and provides reliable income. Because of their high dividends, these stocks are good investments for preretirement and retirement years. The portfolios shown below indicate how preferred issues and other investments are appropriate for your preretirement portfolio.

Bull Market

Objectives	Preserve capital and receive high reliable income with low risk
Risk Levels	Very low for preferred issues; low for fund with blend of large growth and value stocks; very low for utility stocks and fund
Suggestions	Preferred issues, 25 percent
	Utilities stocks or fund, 25 percent
	Barclays fund that tracks the S&P 500 index of blend of large growth and value companies, symbol IVV, 50 percent

Range-Bound Market

Objectives	Preserve capital and receive reliable income with low risk
Risk Levels	Very low for preferred issues; low for utility stocks and fund; low for REIT fund
Suggestions	Preferred issues, 30 percent
	Utility stocks and fund, 20 percent
	REIT fund, 50 percent

Bear Market

Objectives	Preserve capital and receive high income with low risk
Risk Levels	Very low for money market fund; none for zero coupon bond; very low for preferred issues; very low for utility stocks and fund
Suggestions	One-year term U.S. zero coupon bonds 50 percent
	or
	Brokerage's money market fund, 50 percent
	Preferred issues, 40 to 50 percent
	Utility stocks and fund, 0 to 10 percent

Chapter 13

Portfolio Management for Ages 60 Plus

Introduction

This is another transitional phase. During these preretirement years, it's important to conduct several reviews of your progress toward your financial goal. These reviews will help you decide the timing of your retirement. If you started this plan when you were young and made prudent selections of investments, your accumulated assets will allow you to retire on schedule and in good style.

Once retired, it is essential to preserve those assets to maintain your purchasing power against the erosion caused by inflation or the expenses of health problems associated with old age. The Federal Reserve Board's policy regarding inflation is to hold it around the level of 2 percent per year. The Chairman and the other voting members of the Federal Reserve believe this amount of inflation is necessary to keep the economy expanding. Due to this belief and the policy of accepting inflation, your assets will be eroded after your retirement if you do not take preventive action. While a 2 percent rate of inflation doesn't seem like much, it will erode 20 percent of your purchasing power in 10 years. Unless you protect yourself against inflation, you won't be able to maintain the lifestyle you want.

Another potentially large drain on your assets is the negative financial impact of a serious illness if one afflicts you or your family. Government health agencies are projecting large increases in the incidence of chronic diseases. Taking action to deal with the related financial concerns will enable you to preserve your wealth and purchasing power. The investments that can protect your assets against inflation and serious sickness are Treasury Inflation-Protected Securities (TIPS) and long-term care insurance.

Treasury Inflation-Protected Securities

Treasury Inflation-Protected Securities are an investment whose principal and payments are adjusted to compensate for inflation as measured by the Consumer Price Index (CPI). The interest rate is constant, but generates a different payment amount when multiplied by changes in the inflation-adjusted CPI. This provides you with a hedge against inflation because it preserves your purchasing power as the CPI rises. TIPS are offered to the public by the U.S. Treasury Department in 5-, 10-, and 20-year maturities. Interest payments to investors are made semi-annually. TIPS can be bought directly from the government at Treasurydirect.gov.

An investment in these securities can also be made through a traditional or Internet brokerage. To do this you could buy an exchange-traded fund with the symbol TIP. This fund, which is managed by Lehman Brothers investment bank, pays dividends when inflation is rising as represented by the Consumer Price Index. It also distributes capital gains, if any, at the end of the year.

Long-Term Wealth Protection

In order to protect your purchasing power, you must preserve your assets. If you remain in good health while retired, this will not be difficult. But if you or a family member contracts a chronic, incapacitating disease, the massive increase in expenses can decimate your wealth. Nursing home and hospital stays cost thousands of dollars a month and in-home nursing care can also be very expensive. Long-term care insurance policies are designed to pay most of those expenses for you. Take the time now to educate yourself about these policies. The companies offering these policies have restrictions in regard to preexisting illnesses. Waiting until symptoms are obvious would cause your application to be rejected. A long-term care policy would protect your assets and could become one of the best investments you ever make.

Review of Investment Choices

During the course of this lifetime plan, you have learned about a wide variety of investment vehicles. To assist you in making the decisions

Investment Type	Main Features
Barclays funds that track S&P indexes	Opportunity for capital gains during bull markets. Diversified for low risk.
Money market funds	Safety of principal. The fund appreciates over time.
U.S. zero coupon bonds	Safety of principal. You receive a capital gain upon maturity.
National muni bond funds	High monthly income. Low risk.
Investment-grade bond funds	High monthly income. Low risk.
Preferred issues	Safety of principal. High income. They are similar to bonds.
Real estate investment trust funds	High income. Potential for funds capital gain.
Utility stocks and funds	Reliable income in all types of markets. Potential for capital gain.
Treasury Inflation-Protected Securities	Protection against inflation via payments based on rises in the Consumer Price Index.
Lehman Brothers fund (TIP)	Protection against inflation. Dividend payments are made each month the Consumer Price Index rises.
Long-term care insurance	Protection against financial drain of chronic, incapacitating diseases.

about which investments to choose in the years ahead, see the above review of their characteristics.

Transition into Retirement Portfolio

In the display below is a summary of the portfolio from the preceding five-year time period. This is the starting investment posture from which you will make your transition into your retirement portfolio. With the list above as your reference, make your investments on the basis of your desire for additional capital gains, your need for income and your tolerance of risk.

Bull Market	
Suggestion	Barclays S&P 500 blended fund, symbol IVV, 50 percent
	Preferred issues, 25 percent
	Utilities, 25 percent
Range-Bound Market	
Suggestions	REIT fund, 50 percent
	Preferred issues, 30 percent
	Utility stocks, 20 percent
Bear Market	
Suggestions	Brokerage's money market fund
	or
	U.S. zero coupon bonds, 50 percent
	Preferred stocks, 40 to 50 percent
	Utility stocks, 0 to 10 percent

Chapter 14

*Portfolio Management
in Retirement*

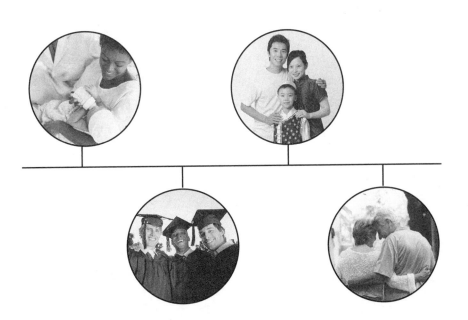

Introduction

You are now at a major decision point. Based on the size of your portfolio and other considerations, you need to decide whether to continue investing actively or be satisfied with the income you are receiving from your investments. Here are some questions to help you make that decision.

- Will the projected income from your portfolio provide you with the lifestyle you want?
- Do you enjoy the activities involved in making investments?
- Do you have a continuing interest in the stock market?
- Are you willing to spend some time doing research to find investment opportunities?
- Are you prepared to take some risk to increase the value of your portfolio?

Depending on your answers to those questions, make your decision as to whether you will continue to be an active investor or reduce your activity to a minimum. In either case, this chapter offers some guidance on how to manage your portfolio during retirement.

Active Investing in Retirement

Some longtime investors do not stop investing after they retire. Some who have been successful want to continue looking for capital gains. Others want to increase their income. Some keep playing the game to avoid boredom. Some enjoy the excitement of finding a company with great prospects as yet undiscovered by the investment community. And some are risk-tolerant successful investors who enjoy the challenges presented by the stock market. If one or more of these comments apply, you may decide to stay active in the market.

If you keep participating, it is most important to play by the following rules to protect what you have acquired. Conduct a thorough investigation of the fundamental and technical condition of each investment before you buy. (Chapters 1 and 2 provide the guidelines for doing this.) Don't be tempted by advertisements suggesting that you buy stocks described as "Hot." Those stocks usually cool off fast without warning. Buy the leading company in a growing industry and avoid the weaker competitors. Adjust the contents of your portfolio to adapt to each change in the phase of the market. And most important, maintain a diversified portfolio to keep the risk level low.

Investment Choices for Bull and Range-Bound Markets

You are now familiar with the variety of investments that were described in earlier chapters. You are also knowledgeable about the objectives you should aim for. These are to preserve capital while seeking some gains; to ensure the continuation of a reliable income stream; and to achieve a low level of risk by diversifying across asset classes. It will be up to you to make specific selections based on your research. It will also be your decision as to what percent of your portfolio will be devoted to each investment. Here are some appropriate types of investments to preserve capital, maintain income flow, and keep the level of risk low.

1. Treasury Inflation-Protected Securities (TIPS)
   These are available in $1,000 units to mature in 5, 10, or 20 years. The principal is guaranteed by the U.S. Treasury. They pay interest every 6 months. Payments rise with the rate of inflation as measured by the Consumer Price Index.
   Examples: See list of TIPS in *Barron's* magazine in the bonds section under the heading of "Inflation-Indexed Trea-

sury Securities." They can be bought through your brokerage or from the U.S. Treasury Department at Treasurydirect.com. Or you can buy the Lehman Brothers TIPS bond fund. The symbol is TIP. The fund pays dividends when inflation is rising as represented by changes in the Consumer Price Index. This fund also distributes capital gains, if any, once a year.

2. Real Estate Investment Trust (REIT) funds

   These funds invest in real estate. Their revenues come from leasing their properties. REIT funds are required to pay out 90 percent of their net income to shareholders. Some capital gain is possible if prices of their properties rise.

   Example: Cohen & Steers Advantage fund pays a dividend of approximately 7 percent. The symbol is RLF. See Chapter 6 for additional REIT funds.

3. Preferred Issues

   The return of principal is promised by the issuing corporation. Dividend rates are higher than that of the common stock. A capital gain is possible if the preferred issue is purchased at less than $25 par value.

   Example: Equity Residential Properties (Symbol EQR, issue D) pays a dividend of approximately 8 percent. See Chapter 12 for additional preferred issues.

4. Utility Companies

   Their revenues are highly reliable. Their dividends rise over time as they increase the charges for their services.

   Example: Great Plains Energy Inc., pays a dividend of approximately 5 percent. The symbol is GXP. See Chapter 11 for additional utility stocks.

5. S&P index of 500 large companies selected for value.

   Example: Barclays iShares S&P 500 fund that tracks the performance of the S&P index of 500 large value stocks, symbol IVE.

Bear Market Investments

Your bear market investments should emphasize the preservation of capital and the elimination of risk. The key to preserving capital during a bear market is to recognize it at the beginning by noting when the S&P index of 500 stocks drops through its 200-day moving average. When this happens, consider the following investments to preserve capital and reduce risk to the lowest level.

1. Zero coupon bonds are an effective, no-risk way to preserve your capital. They are available in units of $1,000 and are bought at a discount. You receive face value at maturity or they can be sold before maturity to provide cash.

2. Preferred issues provide high income flow. The issuing corporation pays dividends quarterly and promises return of par value if the stock is ever called. Check QuantumOnline.com to get the details on any preferred stock of interest to you.

3. Brokerage money market funds provide a temporary place to invest the proceeds from the sale of your bull market investments. Some brokerages sweep the proceeds into their money market funds automatically after sales have been made. Check with your brokerage and make the arrangement to have this done.

Inactive Retirement Investing

Minimum activity investing can be achieved by the traditional buy and hold strategy. Here are some types of investments and specific suggestions to implement this approach.

1. Lehman Brothers fund which holds Treasury Inflation-Protected Securities can be bought on the New York Stock Exchange using the symbol TIP. These will provide protection against rises in the Consumer Price Index.

2. Many corporations issue preferred stocks. Some of these stocks are listed in Chapter 12. From those and from the list below, select several preferred issues as long-term investments. Preferred stocks paying high dividends can provide a steady stream of income to meet living expenses.

Company and Symbol	Dividend Rate
Ace, Ltd. (ACE-C)	7%
Goldman Sachs (GS-B)	6%
Vornado Realty Trust (VNO-F)	6%

If you do research to find additional preferred stocks, look for those that are issued by a company with an established position in an industry that provides products and services essential to our modern style of living. Make sure the preferred issue carries an investment grade rating of AAA, AA, A, or BBB. Find the ratings at QuantumOnline.com. Dividends are paid quarterly for as long as you hold a stock or until it is called.

3. Investment grade bond funds are a reliable source of monthly income. These funds are listed in Barron's magazine in the Closed-End Fund section. Three of these funds that sell at a discount to net asset value and pay high quarterly dividends are listed here.
   - John Hancock Income Fund, symbol JHS
   - Hartford Income, symbol HSF
   - BlackRock Core Bond Trust, symbol BHK

4. World equity funds provide geographic diversification which lowers the level of risk. These funds should benefit from the process of globalization which will result in long-term economic growth worldwide. As emerging economies continue to develop, those parts of the world will produce financial re-

wards for global investors. These funds have the objectives of capital gains and income. They pay dividends monthly. Four of these funds are listed here.

- BlackRock Global Opportunities Equity Trust, symbol BOE
- Calamos Global Total Return fund, symbol CGO
- Eaton Vance Tax Advantaged Global Dividend Income fund, symbol ETG
- Lazard Global Total Return and Income fund, symbol LGI

5. Real estate investment trust funds are another source of monthly income. They are required to pay 90 percent of their income to stockholders. Three of these funds are
- RMR Real Estate Fund, symbol RMR
- Cohen & Steers Premium Income Realty fund, symbol RPF
- Neuberger Berman Real Estate Securities Income Fund, symbol NRO

Additional REIT funds are listed in Chapter 6.

NOTE

Summary portfolios will not be suggested because it is more appropriate for you to select investments on the basis of your personal need for income, your level of risk tolerance, and the limit of your comfort zone. However, if you want a suggestion to help you get started, your initial portfolio could be divided as follows:

- Preferred issues paying high dividends, 40 percent
- Investment grade bond fund paying monthly dividends, 20 percent
- World equity fund paying monthly dividends, 20 percent
- Real estate investment trust fund paying high dividends, 10 percent

- Lehman Brothers inflation protection fund, symbol TIP, 10 percent

Some Final Suggestions

When you are ready to retire, staying in good health is the best way to enjoy your golden years. Here are a few suggestions to help you stay healthy.

- Stay active mentally and read educational literature. Also, play chess, checkers, scrabble, bridge, and other games that require concentration. If you can't find local players, the Internet has many Web sites that offer these activities.
- Stay active physically. Play tennis; go dancing or take dance lessons; take walks in the park; plant a garden; go for bicycle rides; go swimming or do exercises in the pool; join a health club or an aerobic exercise group, or engage in any other form of regular physical activity.
- Get active in your community. Do some volunteer work for the Red Cross; the Scouts of America; a Little League baseball team; a soccer league, or any other local organization.
- Above all, practice healthful habits. Don't smoke; don't drink excessively; keep your weight under control; with your doctor's approval, take a salmon oil supplement to maintain the health of your cardiovascular system; avoid sunbathing in the middle of the day; take naps; patronize your local health food store.

By following these suggestions, you improve your chances of staying healthy so you can enjoy the retirement you have been working for.

Appendix A

Overview of Lifespan Investing

It's important that you set an achievable goal that is in line with your level of motivation, the time you have available, the effort you are willing to make, and the risk level you feel comfortable with. A summary of the life spanning investment strategy is presented below. By reviewing it once in a while, you can ensure that you stay within the framework of the plan. The guides reflect the three phases of the market you will have to deal with.

Guide for a Bull Market

Age Range	Objectives	Suggested Investments	Level of Risk
20–35	Superior capital gains	Small growth stocks	Elevated
		Small stock fund	Low
35–50	Superior capital gains and high income	Medium-sized growth stocks	Elevated
		Medium-sized stock fund	Low
50 to retired	Preserve capital and receive high income	Preferred issues with high dividends	Very low
		Utility stocks or fund	Low
		Large-sized stock fund	Low
Retirement (Inactive investor)	Capital preservation and high income	High dividend preferred issues	Very low
		Investment-grade bond fund	Low
		World equity fund	Low
		REIT	Low
		TIPS (symbol TIP)	None

Guide for a Range-Bound Market

Age Range	Objectives	Suggested Investments	Level of Risk
20–35	High income with some capital gains	Small growth stocks	Elevated
		Small stock fund	Low
		REIT fund	Low
35–50	High income with some capital gains	Medium-sized growth stocks	Elevated
		REIT fund	Low
		High dividend preferred stocks	Very low
50–Retire	Preserve capital and receive high income	High dividend preferred stocks	Very low
		REIT fund	Low
		High dividend utility stocks	Low
Retirement (Inactive investor)	Capital preservation and receive high income	High dividend preferred stocks	Very low
		Investment-grade bond fund	Low
		World equity fund	Low
		REIT fund	Low
		TIPS (symbol TIP)	None

Guide for a Bear Market

Age Range	Objectives	Suggested Investments	Level of Risk
20–35	Preserve capital and receive income	Money market	Very low
		Zero coupon bonds	None
35–50	Preserve capital and receive income	Money market	Very low
		Zero coupon bonds	None
50–65	Preserve capital and receive income	Money market	Very low
		Preferred issues	Very low
		Utility stocks or fund	Very low
		Zero coupon bonds	None
Retirement (Inactive investor)	Preserve capital and receive high income.	High dividend preferred issues	Very low
		Investment-grade bond fund	Low
		World equity fund	Low
		REIT fund	Low
		TIPS (symbol TIP)	None

Appendix B

Glossary

Accumulation Persistent purchases of a stock by knowledgeable investors who believe the shares are greatly underpriced. This activity takes place as a rounding bottom is forming.

Annual Report Every company listed on a stock exchange must publish an audited report on its financial condition and operational results after the end of its fiscal year.

Asset Allocation Dividing one's financial resources among different classes of investments such as stocks, bonds, mutual funds, commodities, and real estate.

At the Market A term that can be used in entering a buy or sell order. It requires the order to be executed immediately.

Average Trading Volume The average number of shares traded over the previous months. This figure is recalculated every business day by eliminating the oldest day's trading volume and adding the most recent day's volume.

Bear Market A phrase that describes a market phase during which most stock prices are trending downward for an extended time. Upward price movements in comparison are shorter in time and length. During this phase, the market averages display a series of descending short-term tops.

Blended Fund A fund that has stocks of companies whose businesses and stock prices are growing rapidly. It also has stocks of companies that are undervalued by virtue of having price-to-earnings ratios much lower than others in the industry.

Bottom Fishing Making a purchase during a long downtrend. The buyer hopes to buy at the bottom price, but the chance of catching the bottom using this tactic is extremely remote.

Bottoming Out A process by which a downtrend is changed into an uptrend. This can occur quickly by means of a breakout from a downtrend, or in a key reversal day. Or it can develop over an extended time in the form of a major bottom pattern. (*See* Bottom Pattern.)

Bottom Pattern   There are three common bottom patterns that occur at major bottoms: rounding bottom, double bottom, and inverted head and shoulders. Variations on these patterns and ill-defined formations can also occur at bottoms.

Breakout   *See* Downside Breakout *and* Upside Breakout.

Brokerage   A company in the business of acting as an agent in the purchase and sale of stocks and bonds and other financial instruments.

Bulletin Board   The companies listed here do not meet the reporting requirements of the major exchanges. The lack of official information on them makes them subject to rumors and manipulation schemes.

Bull Market   A phrase that describes the stock market when most prices are trending upward for an extended time period. Downward price movements in comparison are shorter in time and length. During this phase the market averages display a pattern of rising short-term bottoms.

Business Model   A viable business is one that generates revenues in excess of costs and expenses resulting in a profitable operation. A prudent investor makes the effort to find out if this is being accomplished on a consistent basis.

Buying on Margin   Borrowing money from the brokerage to buy stocks or other investments.

Call Date   The date on, or after, which a bond or a preferred stock may be redeemed by the issuer.

Call Price   The amount of money the purchaser of a bond or preferred stock will receive when the investment is redeemed.

Capital Gain   The amount of profit on a completed transaction.

Capital Loss   The amount of loss on a completed transaction.

Capitulation   The selling of stocks that occurs at the bottom of a long decline in a bear market. The emotional component of this selling activity is despair and panic.

Churn an Account   Unjustified trading by a broker for the primary purpose of increasing commissions.

Closed-End Fund   A fund that issues a limited number of shares that can be traded like stocks.

Commission   A fee charged by brokerages to execute a trade on behalf of a customer.

Common Stock   The basic form of ownership in a corporation which entitles the holder to voting rights and a proportionate share of dividends.

Consolidation   The price action of a stock fluctuating within a trading range as a preparation for a move to higher levels.

Continuation Pattern   The price action of a stock fluctuating within a triangle before breaking out of the pattern to proceed in the same direction. If the price was falling before entering the pattern, its exit is to the downside. If the price was rising before entry, its exit is to the upside.

Cover a Short Sale   To sell short, shares are borrowed from an individual through a brokerage. After the sale is made, an equal number of shares must be returned to the lender. Covering the short sale is the act of buying shares on the market and returning them to the lender.

Cyclical Industry   An industry whose earnings rise and fall as a result of the rise and fall of the economy.

Day Trader   A speculator who watches the market action and often makes one or more transactions within a business day.

Debt Level   The amount of money owed by the company. As the ratio of debt to assets rises, the company becomes increasingly vulnerable to bankruptcy.

Defensive Stocks   Stocks whose prices resist the declines caused by economic recessions. These stocks have reliable earnings and pay high dividends.

Demand   The total number of shares sought for purchase by all buyers. When this amount exceeds the number of shares offered for sale, the price rises.

Discount   The amount of money paid by a buyer below the par value or the net asset value of the security.

Discount Brokerage   A brokerage that provides transaction services at commissions that are less than those charged by full service, traditional brokerages.

Discretionary Account   An account where an investor gives control to the broker. The broker can then buy and sell without the approval of the customer. A discretionary account is a very high risk situation because the investor depends on the broker to be completely trustworthy, competent, and totally devoid of conflicts of interest.

Distribution   Persistent selling of shares by knowledgeable stockholders who are aware that prices are unjustifiably high. This activity occurs at the top of a bull phase in the market as a rounding top is forming.

Diversification   The spreading of investments among a variety of asset classes to control the overall risk level of the portfolio.

Dividend   The dollar amount paid to each stockholder from the earnings of the company.

Dividend Rate   The amount of the yearly dividend expressed as a percent of the share price.

Double Bottom   The price pattern formed when the stock price makes a bottom, rises to a short-term top, returns to the approximate level of the previous bottom, and subsequently rises beyond the short-term top.

Double Top   The price pattern formed when the stock price rises to a top, falls to a short-term bottom, returns to the approximate level of the previous top, and subsequently falls below the previous short-term bottom.

Downside Breakout   A price drop through a support level or down through a moving average of the stock price. A downside breakout is a sell signal because it implies a move to much lower prices.

Downtrend Line   A line drawn through two or more descending short-term tops.

Due Diligence   The conduct of a thorough investigation into fundamental value and timeliness of the purchase before making an investment.

Earnings Growth Rate   The percentage at which a company's net income is growing year over year.

Emerging Market   A country which has had an agrarian- or resource-based economy, but is adding industries and financial institutions.

Exchange-Traded Funds   These aim to duplicate the performance of an index, a commodity, or a basket of commodities.

Exponential Moving Average   A charted line that represents the average of a consecutive series of prices with extra weight given to the most recent prices.

Full-Service Brokerage   One that provides advice, research information and other services, and charges higher commissions than discount brokerages. Transactions are executed by a broker on behalf of the client.

Fundamental Analysis   The review of company products, services, financial condition, competition, and other basic factors affecting a company's earnings and prospects.

General Obligation Bond   A bond that is issued by a state. Payment of interest and principal is guaranteed by the state.

Globalization   This refers to the movement toward expanding communications, commerce, and cooperation among businesses internationally.

Global Reach   Companies whose brand, products, and services are known and accepted around the world are said to have global reach.

Growth Company   A company that is projected to have superior earnings growth and stock price performance.

Initial Public Offering   The initial offer of shares to the public for purchase from a company through an underwriting investment company, commercial bank, or brokerage. After the offering is completed, the shares trade on a stock exchange.

Intermediate Term   The time period between six months and one year.

Internet Brokerage An online brokerage company that does business through an electronic network.

Inverted Head and Shoulders A major bottoming pattern composed of a bottom, another lower bottom, and a third bottom at a level approximate to the level of the first bottom.

Key Reversal Day A day on which a stock price makes a new high but closes with a loss on large trading volume. The price trend then changes from up to down. Also, a day on which a stock price makes a new low but closes with a gain on large trading volume. The price trend then changes from down to up.

Large Capitalization When the value the market puts on the outstanding shares of a company's stock is more than $10 billion. (*See* Market Capitalization.)

Limit Order Placing an order to buy or sell at the price you specify. If you are buying, the order limits the price you are willing to pay, but allows for you to pay a lower price. If you are selling, the order limits the price you are willing to accept, but allows for you to receive a higher price.

Liquidation Value The price at which a preferred stock is redeemed when it is called or matures.

Long Term A period of time one year or longer.

Margin This is the amount of money a brokerage lends to a customer for the purpose of buying an investment or selling it short. (*See* Margin Call.)

Margin Call If an investor buys or sells on margin and the stock price goes in the losing direction beyond the limit set by the brokerage, it notifies the customer how much more money is needed. If the investor is not able to provide the extra money, the brokerage may make a transaction to limit the loss. The investor is obligated to pay for any losses.

Market Capitalization   This figure is the number of outstanding shares multiplied by the price of the stock.

Market Index   A market index represents the composite price of a group of stocks. For example, the S&P index of 500 stocks represents the price level of those stocks as a group.

Medium Capitalization   When the value the market puts on the company's outstanding stock is between $2 and $10 billion. (*See* Market Capitalization.)

Message Boards   Where mail messages are posted by those interested in the company and its stock. Most of the messages are either promotional or disparaging, depending on whether the person has a long or short position in the stock. It is imprudent to take action based on the content of message boards.

Momentum Player   An active trader who watches for a fast-moving stock and buys or sells it short hoping for a quick capital gain. Succeeding at this game requires excellent timing and nerves of steel.

Morningstar   The premier fund rating service. The best rating is five stars. Only outstanding funds get this rating.

Mortgage-Backed Securities   Some real estate investment trusts assemble mortgages into packages which can then be sold to other companies which buy them for the income they deliver.

Nasdaq   This acronym stands for National Association of Securities Dealers Automated Quotations system. This electronic market system is operated and regulated by the National Association of Security Dealers (NASD).

Net Asset Value Per Share   The market value of a fund's portfolio of stocks and other investments, minus any liabilities, divided by the number of shares issued by the fund.

Net Income Per Common Share   This equals total revenues minus all costs and expenses and any dividends paid on preferred shares.

Objective   (Adjective) Based on hard data and reliable information.

Operating Profit Margin   This equals the percentage obtained by dividing net income by total revenue. The higher this percentage, the more efficiently the company is operating.

Overbought   A security that has become severely overpriced due to excessive demand by eager buyers.

Oversold   A security that has become severely underpriced due to excessive supply offered by anxious sellers.

Paper Loss   A loss that has not been taken and remains in the account.

Paper Profit   A profit that has not been taken and remains in the account.

Parabolic Curve   A charted price increase that accelerates until it is going almost straight up. This rate of rise cannot be sustained. When the demand for the stock has been exhausted, the price falls to much lower levels.

Par Value   The value of a security as established by the issuer.

Pink Sheets   A list of companies that do not meet the financial reporting requirements of the stock exchanges. Bid and ask prices are published once a day. These stocks are generally regarded as very speculative.

Portfolio   The collection of securities an investor accumulates. The contents should be rebalanced as the market moves through the bull, range-bound, and bear phases.

Preferred Stock   A class of stock that takes precedence over common stock in regard to dividend payments. The issuer promises to redeem the stock at par value on or after the call date.

Premium Price   The price paid by a buyer who pays more than the par value of a security or the net asset value per share of a closed-end fund.

Price-to-Book Value   The result of dividing the current closing price by the latest book value per share. For example, if the closing price is $48 and the latest book value per share is $6, the price-to-book value is 8 to1. (Low price-to-book values are better than high ones.)

Price-to-Earnings Ratio   The result of dividing the price of a stock by the earnings per share for the year. For example, if the stock price is $10 and the company earned $1 per share, 10 divided by 1 equals 10 so the price-to-earnings ratio is 10 to 1. (Low price-to- earnings ratios are better than high ones.)

Profit Margin   Equals total revenue minus the cost of goods sold expressed as a percentage of revenues. For example, if total revenue is $1,000,000 and cost of sales is $400,000 the profit margin is $600,000 divided by $1,000,000, which is 60 percent.

Prospectus   A document provided by a company describing its business, objectives, finances, risks, and other information of importance to a prospective investor.

Pump and Dump This is a tactic of unscrupulous stock manipulators. They promote the stock to get the price up beyond its reasonable value. They then sell to take the capital gain.

Range-Bound This refers to a market that lacks the momentum to trend up or down. In this condition the market index vacillates within a limited vertical distance for an indefinite time.

Rebalance To adjust the contents of a portfolio to meet the changing conditions of the stock market as it moves through bull, range-bound, and bear phases.

REIT Acronym for real estate investment trust. Most of these trusts own real properties and lease them to generate income. Some REITs deal in mortgages rather than real properties.

Relative Strength The rating of a stock's price performance relative to the performance of other stocks. A rating above 50 is a sign of strength. A rating below 50 indicates weakness.

Resistance Level The price level from which a stock's price has declined in past attempts to rise above it.

Risk Averse This term applies to investors who avoid high risk investments. Taking on high risk makes a risk averse investor uncomfortable which can lead to making unwise decisions.

Risk Tolerance The level of risk an investor is able to tolerate comfortably for the opportunity to make capital gains.

Rounding Bottom The saucer-shaped curve that develops when a stock price in a downtrend gradually changes into an uptrend.

Rounding Top A curving top formation that develops when an uptrend is converted gradually into a downtrend.

Securities and Exchange Commission (SEC)   The federal agency with the authority to regulate the actions of companies listed on the stock exchanges.

Selling Short   The sale of borrowed shares in the hope the price will decline. The seller would then buy them back at the lower price, return them to the lender, and profit from the price difference. This is a very risky action because there's no limit on how high the price might go, making the potential loss also unlimited.

Service Provider   A technology company that connects personal computers to the Internet and provides a variety of information services and access to thousands of Web sites. This type of service is essential for investors who use an Internet brokerage.

Short Squeeze   The situation that develops when a stock which has been sold short by many speculators rises to price levels that scare the short sellers and pressures them to buy back the stock as the price rise continues.

Short Term   A time period up to six months.

Simple Moving Average   An average calculated from a consecutive series of preceding daily closing prices.

Small Capitalization   The value the market puts on the company's outstanding stock is between $200 million and $2 billion. (*See* Market Capitalization.)

Spot Price   The price to buy a commodity for immediate delivery.

Standard & Poor's Corporation   A company that maintains several market indexes. It also provides bond and preferred stock ratings to the investment community.

Supply The total number of shares stockholders want to sell. When this number is much larger than the amount investors want to buy, the price declines.

Support Level The level from which a stock price has risen one or more times.

Sustainable Angle of Ascent Angles of ascent between 10 and 30 degrees are sustainable for the long term. Angles of ascent between 30 and 45 degrees are sustainable for the intermediate term. Angles of ascent above 45 degrees are sustainable for the short term.

Technical Analysis The interpretation of stock price patterns and trading volume data to project stock price movements and identify when to buy, how long to hold, and when to sell.

Topping Out The process by which an uptrend is converted into a downtrend. This can occur quickly by a downward penetration of an uptrend line. Or it can take an extended period of time while a major top develops.

Trading Platform This is an order entry service provided by Internet brokerages. The platform provides data processing to give the investor the information needed to make trading decisions.

Trailing Stop Loss Order Traders and investors use these orders to preserve capital. The order is raised after each higher price move. When the price declines to the price specified in the order, it becomes an order to sell at the market.

Underwrite This is the activity required to prepare for the offering of an investment to investors. These preparations are coordinated by an investment bank or another qualified financial institution.

Upside Breakout A rise through a resistance level or up through a downtrending moving average of the stock price. This penetration is usually followed by a price move to higher levels if the breakout is accompanied by a large increase in trading volume.

Uptrend Line A line drawn through two or more ascending short-term bottoms.

Value Investment A stock that has a price-to-earnings ratio that is much lower than other stocks in the same industry.

Yield The amount of return on a stock when dividends and capital gains or losses are added together. For bonds, it is the return when interest and capital gains or losses are added together.

Zero Coupon Bond A bond that has been stripped of its interest coupons and makes no interest payments. These bonds are bought at a discount and the buyer receives par value when the bond matures. The return to the holder is the dollar amount of the discount when the bond is purchased.

Appendix C

Internet Resources

The Web sites described here present information that can help you make investment decisions. Most of the content of these sites is available without charge. When the market is open, prices are updated immediately. Millions of investors visit these sites during a single business day. An investor who does not use these resources is laboring under a large disadvantage. These sites contain a wealth of information, and the following descriptions only serve as a brief preview you can expand on when you have time available.

NOTE

The format and services provided by Web sites are subject to change. Consequently, you will not always be able to follow the research procedures in the text exactly as they are written. If this happens, try to find an alternative procedure or a different Web site that provides the information you are searching for.

StockCharts

URL address: stockcharts.com

This site features a variety of stock charts designed to assist technical analysis. At the home page click on the drop down menu and select "Gallery View." After entering a stock symbol in the search slot and clicking "Go," you will have access to two stock price charts with moving averages, trading volume, and the current stock price. This site also features a study curriculum accessible under the heading of "Chart School." This is an excellent source for a self-education project to broaden your knowledge of technical analysis.

Yahoo! Finance

URL address: finance.yahoo.com

This site gives you access to a variety of technical and fundamental information and statistics. It provides detailed data on thousands of stocks and funds. Items available from the menu include company profile, income statement, balance sheet, operating profit margin, amount of debt, price-to-earnings ratio, competitors, dividends paid previously, major stockholders, percent of dividend yield, and other statistics. A chart of the history of the stock price and comparisons of the performance of the stock versus that of other stocks and market indexes are available.

ClearStation

URL address: clearstation.com
This site displays price charts on thousands of stocks. It shows a short- and a medium-term moving average for each stock and indicates how far above or below the price is in relation to each average. Other items of interest shown as adjuncts to each chart are dividends, quarterly earnings, and relative strength compared to other stocks. If you want to know when a company will report its quarterly earnings, this is the place to find that information. Another helpful feature of this site is the identification of stocks that are in uptrends. These stocks are shown on the home page in the section labeled "A-List" under the heading "Trending Up." This list changes every day and is a resource for finding stocks with potential for capital gains.

Big Charts

URL address: bigcharts.com
The home page of this service gives the option of three types of charts: "Basic Chart," "Advanced Chart," and "Interactive Chart." Enter a stock symbol in the search slot, click on Basic Chart and click on "1 day" to see a summary of the day's transactions. Beneath that is

a one-year history of the stock price along with the trading volume. You can also call up a profile of the company or fund, analysts' ratings, insider transactions, and recent news items.

"Interactive Chart" allows you to select a time period from one day to ten years, a particular year, or any other past time period. You have the option of comparing the stock price performance against several market indexes. This service also allows you to select your preferred chart features and store them. When you return to the site, they are displayed automatically for your convenience.

MSN Money Central

URL address: moneycentral.msn.com

At the home page click on "Investing" and then click on "Stocks" in the toolbar. A display called "Welcome to Stock Research" appears. To the right, under the heading of "Research Tools" you will see the phrase "StockScouter." Click on this and enter a stock symbol in the search slot. Click "Go" and a numerical rating from 1 to 10 appears. This is the rating of the company as an investment with 10 being the highest. Scroll down and on the right side of the screen under "Expected Risk/Return" is a comparison of risk to return shown in the form of two bars. The length of the bars provides an objective measure of risk versus return for the investment. After comparing the lengths of the two bars, you can decide if the level of risk is within your comfort zone.

QuantumOnline

URL address: quantumonline.com

This site is a comprehensive resource for finding information on issues of preferred stocks. To use this search service, you need to enter the company's stock symbol followed by the letter identifying the preferred issue in this format, ABC-D. The resulting display shows the price at the initial offering, the amount of the dividend, the percent yield to the investor, and whether the dividends are cumulative. It indicates the amount to be paid to the investor if the stock is called. It shows the credit rating for the issue as given by Standard & Poor's rating service.

Although preferred issues are called stocks, they actually are more like bonds because the issuer guarantees the return of the investment when it is called or at maturity. If you want to invest in preferred issues, this is an excellent place to start your research efforts.

MarketWatch from Dow Jones

URL address: marketwatch.com
At the home page click on "Tools & Research." From the menu on the left side of the screen click on "Charts." Enter a stock symbol in the search slot and click on the arrow. A one-year history of the stock price is displayed along with the record of trading volume. Other time periods from one day to five years are available. You can also compare the stock price performance against the S&P index of 500 stocks and other indexes. This site has a wide variety of market-related information. Explore it when you have some time.

Real Estate Investment Trusts (REITs)

URL address: investinreits.com
At the home page click on "REITs by Ticker Symbol." A list of hundreds of REITs is presented by name and ticker symbol. Click on a symbol and the Yahoo! Finance home page appears showing the basic information on that REIT. Additional fundamental and technical information is available from the menu on the left side of the screen. To get the same type of information on a REIT closed-end fund, go back

to the investinreits.com home page and click on "Closed-End Funds." Explore this site to get helpful information on all types of REITs and REIT funds.

SmartMoney Magazine

URL address: smartmoney.com

This web site reports breaking news. On the left side of the screen is a menu featuring the subjects of stocks, funds, the economy, and articles from *SmartMoney* magazine. A helpful feature is a service that allows you to register 10 stocks. Clicking on a registered stock symbol brings up a profile of the company, a chart showing the stock price action for the day, breaking news on the company, a forecast of its earnings, and key statistics on the company's financial condition. This feature keeps you up to date on stocks of interest to you and provides an assessment of a company's prospects.

Investopedia

URL address: investopedia.com

This is a free primary source for definitions of financial terms. Simply go to the site and enter a word or phrase whose meaning you want to learn in the search slot. The search will show the item you have requested and also show related words and phrases. This is an excellent resource for developing a large repertoire of financial concepts.

Appendix D

Bibliography

Cottle, Sidney, *Graham and Dodd's, Security Analysis*, 5th Ed., New York: McGraw-Hill, 1988.

Darst, David M., *The Art of Asset Allocation*, New York: McGraw-Hill, 2003.

Edwards, Robert D., *Technical Analysis of Stock Trends*, 8th Ed., New York: St. Lucie Press, 2001.

Graham, Benjamin, *Security Analysis*, 4th Ed., New York: McGraw-Hill, 1962.

Jiler, William L., *How Charts Can Help You in the Stock Market*, New York: Trendline Publishing, 1962.

Meyer, Thomas A., *The Technical Analysis Course*, 3rd Ed., New York: McGraw-Hill, 2002.

Pistolese, Clifford, *Select Winning Stocks Using Technical Analysis*, New York: McGraw-Hill, 2007.

————, *Technical Analysis for the Rest of Us*, New York: McGraw-Hill, 2006.

Ritchie, John C., *Fundamental Analysis: A Back-to-the-Basics Investment Guide*, New York: McGraw-Hill, 1995.

Thomsett, Michael C., *Getting Started in Fundamental Analysis*, New York: Wiley, 2006.

Tigue, Joseph, *The Standard & Poor's Guide to Long-Term Investing*, New York: McGraw-Hill, 2003.

Note to Reader

I enjoyed writing this book and hope you enjoyed reading it. If you have constructive criticism or any other comments, I would like to receive them. My e-mail address is Cliffwrite@AOL.com. I don't open e-mail from unknown senders. Please enter Life Span in the subject line. You may also want to post your review on Amazon.com. (Click on Books and use Clifford Pistolese as the search words.) Thank you for reading this book and for taking the time to respond.

Clifford Pistolese

Index

About the Author

Clifford Pistolese is a successful investor who has held executive positions with several Standard & Poor's 500 corporations. He is the author of *Using Technical Analysis, Technical Analysis for the Rest of Us,* and *Select Winning Stocks Using Technical Analysis.*